To my sons Jake and Tom

AFRICAN RELATIONS

A Story Set In The Eastern Cape Of South Africa

Mari Bennett

PARTRIDGE
A Penguin Random House Company

To order additional copies of this book, contact
Toll Free 0800 990 914 (South Africa)
+44 20 3014 3997 (outside South Africa)
orders.africa@partridgepublishing.com

www.partridgepublishing.com/africa

Contents

Part One

Part Two

PART ONE

Introduction

"I was born at the foot of the Katberg Mountains" my mother used to say. As a child these very words brought to my mind another world, unreachable from our suburban home in England. I had no expectation that I would ever see the places she spoke of or know much about the life she so nostalgically remembered.

Kathleen Elizabeth Young (nee Petzer) was of Afrikaans origin on her mother's side. That defines all that she has been in her lifetime. The explanation for all her views, both politically and morally is contained in that fact. As a child I accepted it as a norm, but as I grew older found myself at odds with a culture that was largely reviled by the ethical perception in Britain of the 1960's. In the late 60s as a young woman, I went for a while to live in South Africa and saw the true effects of the apartheid regime which had so repulsed the western world. In those years I lost my feelings of pride in the bedrock of my inherited genes.

The simple fact that my mother grew up within a different culture has intrigued me recently. Where was this place "at the foot of the Katberg Mountains"? In all my years of living in and visiting Africa I had never taken the trouble to find out. The anecdotes she has recited again and again over the years sat dead in the water if I didn't go there and discover.

My mother's family originates from the Eastern Cape of South Africa where she was born in a place called Seymour which is so small that it is difficult to find on a modern map. In December 2012 my husband, Jon, and I flew to East London in the Cape during a holiday in Johannesburg where we had attended my cousin's wedding. We only had a few days to spare at the end of a busy month but I felt that this was an important journey for me to make. When we arrived in East London we were lucky enough to be able to borrow a 4x4 vehicle which would enable us to take a trip into the interior of the Eastern Cape. We had been advised to travel to the Hogsback where we would find good accommodation, and from there we could explore the whole area.

After finding a comfortable hotel in the Hogsback, we set off immediately, in the late afternoon, to look for Seymour and followed a road-sign directing us along a rough road. We picked up an African hitchhiker along the way and chatted to him as we approached his home town.

"This is where the white people lived" he said as we drove into the outskirts of Seymour. This, for him, was now a matter of historical significance which had no bearing on how it affected his life in a reformed South Africa. That was guided by a government and an economy which is now part of a world stage. Whatever his view on the effect of apartheid on his country; he gave no opinion.

A shady street bordered by, now mostly derelict, houses and lined by majestic trees and shrubs was the place where my immediate ancestors had lived. I could see the Dutch-style homes and sense the elite flavour of a time long since gone. As we drove through the, now ramshackle, residences and looked out over the African township that has now established itself sprawling over the hillside, I realised that the secrets of my family's past now were hidden and might never be known if someone didn't tell them. I decided to make a record of all that I know of this bygone time.

My mother was right. She was born at the foot of the Katberg Mountains, or more specifically beside the Katberg River which runs a meandering course, bridged many times by the roads that crisscross the area. The hills which surround it appear like spreading skirts on a young girl curtseying. I never could have pictured it without seeing it but having seen it I feel that perhaps I always knew, deep down, how it would be.

On that day, in our four-wheel-drive vehicle, we returned to the Hogsback over a very rough road which took us on the old route over the mountains. This would have been the passage often taken by my young mother and her family. Seeing the astounding scenery was the reward for struggling over a rugged road pitted with deep troughs and gullies.

In the days that followed, Jon and I explored the area with increasing curiosity. We carried sweeties for the black children and took joy in handing them out when we had the chance. It seemed that the Africans we encountered regarded us as a rare sight in those parts, but they gave no particular deference to our race. They took our sweeties, but maintained a dignity which recent political reform has accorded them. Poverty was all around for us to see, but this is their country, we were left in no doubt about that.

We took a little time to visit the museum at Fort Beaufort. This building was established as an officers' mess in 1830 and abandoned by the British military at the end of the Ninth Frontier war. As a museum it is interesting from the point of view that the various rooms which are given over to the history of the area, show fundamentally how the cultural changes over the decades have affected the region. One room is taken up with ancient and rusted weaponry, and another displayed the Dutch-style dress and domestic commodities worn and used by settlers during the 19th century. Within the building, rooms are taken up with poignant images which bring awareness of the injustices perpetrated by the apartheid era, and the unhappy prison experiences of Steve Biko and Nelson Mandela. It is strange to see signs which declare 'Whites only', long-since removed from benches and public conveniences, now inviting ridicule in the dusty archives of a museum.

Some details were of particular interest to me. Alice was where my grandmother was born and Fort Hare, built as a fortification for the British Army, became a University and the alma mater of Nelson Mandela. Woburn Village has strong links with Xhosa traditions of nationhood and there the Christmas Day memorial commemorates where Xhosa tribes attacked clusters of villages around Alice, allowing women and children to seek safe passage to Fort Hare. The Hogsback had been the headquarters of Xhosa Chief Ngquika, father of Maquoma who fought persistently for the rights of his tribe against the British army. The Katberg Mountains have particular spiritual significance for the Xhosa tribe and link directly with their past. Their clashes with the British government over differences in culture and ways in which land and cattle were valued continued for more than fifty years.

A press photograph showed a smiling General J.C. Smuts as Minister of Justice and Deputy Prime Minister, on Dingaans Day in 1933, posing on the Commonage at Fort Beaufort with the Mayor and Councillors. There was a promise made that the government would take over the expenditure on "Jointed Cactus eradication" and there would be an extension of the mental hospital on a new site. These photographs indicate the local events of particular importance to the white community when my mother was a little girl.

I read with interest the synopsis regarding the small town of Balfour displayed on one wall of the museum. This was described as a place in which whites and blacks had a common vested interest and from the earliest times of colonial settlement had become a cultural melting pot. In 1828 ordnance granted people of mixed ancestry limited land rights and people of all races started to migrate to the area. This would tie in with stories of the very egalitarian attitude of my grandmother, Hester, who is said to have spoken the Xhosa language so well that, if you heard her talking to African people with your back turned, you would not know it was a white woman speaking. She had been brought up within a rural community where harmony and trust were valued aspects of their existence.

By the end of four days, our journey had taken us to Seymour, Alice, Fort Beaufort and Balfour ending at the Hogsback. We travelled back along the well-tarred road to East London, gratefully returned the vehicle which had given us so much opportunity, and flew up to Johannesburg before returning to the UK. We had taken many photographs and my head was buzzing with questions.

At her home in Christchurch, England, I sat with my mother and the photographs we had taken flashed up on to the computer screen one after the other. She peered closely, and sometimes it was necessary to replay an image for her to take a better look.

"Oh yes!" she exclaimed with recognition, time and again. "That was my school, and my father went there too! That used to be the Dutch Reform Church where my mother played the organ! That building is where I dropped and broke my china-faced doll on Christmas Day!"

My mother told me that I had seen what the essence of her early life was. I could now be satisfied that the story I hoped to write would truly capture what can't be changed by time or circumstances. I know what that place in Africa looks like. I understand how the light falls on the hills. I have felt the dust rise on a warm wind and heard the rustle of that African grass. The chill of mountain air and the abundance of bright flowers have given me an understanding of the huge contrasts and variety in the Cape where my mother grew up. Most importantly, I have seen those Katberg Mountains.

Chapter 1

From the time that Jan van Riebeck, the famous Dutch explorer, arrived in Table Bay, Cape Town, in 1652, the course was set. This land would have a rural identity; useful in supplying the ships which travelled to the East Indies. Initially regarded as a harbour and stopping-off point during, what was undoubtedly, a difficult passage from Europe around the Cape of Good Hope towards the East Indies, it was seen that introducing colonists as farmers would be a financially sound strategy. Production of foodstuffs at the lowest possible cost to the Dutch East Indies Company was the original purpose of the introduction of white immigrants.

It has always been contended by my mother that her Dutch descendants had been "kicked out of" Java, in Indonesia. Although I have no way of substantiating this, it could well be that they were amongst the elite Dutch families living in Java, displaced as a result of defeat by the British when they invaded the island in 1811 during the Napoleonic wars, and transported by ship to the new colony in the Cape.

Cloves and nutmeg had gained an enormous value as medicine and food spices in Europe by the 17th century, and definitely worth the dangerous and unpredictably cruel passages undertaken by Dutch ships. It is said that, on some voyages, nearly all of the crew died from accidents, illness or battles with pirates, but for those who survived there were large rewards.

Introducing settlers to the Cape was seen as a way of improving the success of these voyages by providing fresh produce and five years later an experiment was undertaken, by the Company, giving a tax free land bond for 12 years to the Burghers supplying their agricultural needs.

By the beginning of the 18th century the Directors of the Company had opened up cattle trade with the local Hottentots and, as this was creating disruption and competitive unrest among the Dutch Burghers, immigration was later discouraged. White colonists were starting to integrate and French and German immigrants were adding to the mix.

Dispersal of Burghers into the Cape region was encouraged as they were belligerent in nature, and had begun to create more problems than they solved for the Dutch East Indies Company. With their desire for the freedom to own pastoral land and benefit themselves and their families, these hardy farmers pressed further into the interior and played a large part in the changing frontiers of the Cape. By 1775 cattle farmers, seeking better grazing and with an unlimited freedom to roam this fertile countryside, had pushed the frontier from the Breede River where there territories had been set, westwards to the Fish River. In 1778 the Governor of the Cape visited the frontier and found Bantu tribesmen and European farmers living in close proximity to one another, not always harmoniously.

The conflicts that followed between the European settlers and the Xhosa tribe, was complicated by the fact that each held fundamentally different ideas on the holding of land. Where the Europeans regarded land as something that could be bought as property to be inherited by their offspring, Xhosa chiefs did not hold the power to cede or sell their ancestral land. The chiefs in the area were persuaded by the Governor of the Cape that the Fish River should be the boundary between black and white farmers and in 1780 after the first of the Frontier Wars (known as Kaffir Wars at the time), the Council of Policy ratified the agreement and the Xhosa were driven back across the Fish River.

This opened up a new chapter in South African history and was the place where my mother's ancestors settled. At first the wealth of both African and European farmers lay in their cattle and sheep and their sole object in life was to search for more and better water and pastures. Professor W.M. Macmillan said famously: "The little understood Kaffir Wars are probably to be regarded as the struggle between two streams of colonisers for the possession of valuable land". This was all very well, but for five decades the Xhosa tribes in the region resisted the ceding of their ancestral land around the Kat River. In 1795 when the first British occupation started the Army proceeded to create a long chain of fortifications to protect the settlers against aggression from tribesmen.

In 1809 Lieutenant-Colonel Richard, who was in charge of the army at that time, recommended a neutral belt between the Fish and Keiskama Rivers as a result of tribal encroachment on the colony, and to help the situation from the European point of view, 6000 settlers were brought into the area from Britain to increase the density of whites in the frontier districts. The region became known as British Kaffraria.

The British immigrants, who had arrived in South Africa in 1820, mostly settled in the Zuurveld, later known as the Albany District. This was the region between Bushman's River and Fish River from Grahamstown to the coast. They were a formidable group of people, already used to hardship on the high seas, who arrived in the Cape, now ready to establish a life in this inhospitable land without looking back towards an easier life in Europe. Evidence shows that their spirit of community got them through the early days and they shared with their existing Dutch neighbours the hardships of their chosen lifestyle. The British settlers confronted the warring Xhosa tribes with a bravery that they had always been prepared to display. Stories of savage tribes and wild animals had not deterred them. The reward was an opportunity to bring up their children where they could roam free and farm the land. An opportunity which was not available to them in the country they had left behind.

This is, undoubtedly, the stock that my great-grandmother, Petzer, originated from. She was, apparently, a "very educated lady" and the little evidence available shows that she experienced serious nostalgia for England, if not delusions of grandeur. She had ten children and is said to have named them all after the British monarchy. Although 'Francis, Louis, Robert and Sarah' are not names that immediately bring to mind the royal ancestry, 'Charles, Mary, Elisabeth, Arthur and Edward' however can claim to have royal implications and when she died in childbirth, her dying wish that the little girl be named 'Maud', indicates a certain enlightened knowledge of an obscure queen who reigned in English history. Without doubt her wish was to establish that the very English nature of her heritage was acknowledged in the naming of her children.

A year after the 1820 Settlers arrived, the treaty which had established a neutral belt in the territory was reversed and the Xhosa tribe was allowed to return to the valley of the Kat River. This introduces Chief Maquoma to the rich story of the region.

This was a chief who bore the shame of his father, Chief Ngquka, who had negotiated the ceding of the spiritual homeland of the Xhosa to the British government. On becoming chief himself he set up resistance among his tribesmen and with spears and stolen guns they embarked on guerrilla tactics to frustrate and often ambush the British Army. Incursions were sometimes bloody but the Xhosa people see this time in their history as a defending of their heritage rights, and nine, so-called 'frontier wars', are now known by them as the 'wars of dispossession'. During that time the British army burned Xhosa villages, took possession of crops and cattle and created starvation. This created a period of roller-coaster behaviour first of forgiveness then of misunderstanding between the white and black populations. When the Xhosa were allowed to trade in ivory, gum, hides and basket-ware, a mutually lucrative understanding was reached for a period. However in 1834 the Xhosa were again expelled from the territory, and Maquoma, frustrated and angry, was known to have said; "When shall I and my people be able to get rest?"

and this loaded question marked the start of the sixth frontier war. Maquoma and his brother Tyhali at the head of 12 000 Xhosa tribesmen ravaged the European colony as far west as Grahamstown. They destroyed 400 farms and captured thousands of cattle and sheep. Over a hundred Settlers and their Hottentot servants were killed. The British Army under the leadership of Colonel Smith drove the Xhosa back across the Fish, Keiskama and Kei Rivers and Maquoma was captured. It seems that he was sent to Robben Island where a future leader, a man born in the vast region of the Eastern Cape, Nelson (Mandiba) Mandela would also be incarcerated 130 years later.

At Fort Willshire under the control of Colonel Smith a new treaty was drawn up and signed by Maquoma. The Xhosa were allowed then to return to the area under the understanding that blacks would be resettled in allotted reserves and subject to the laws of the Colony. African people were to be regarded as British subjects and their customs adapted for the purposes of administering the reserves. The idea, according to Professor Macmillan, in his paper *Bantu, Boer and Briton*, was to "govern and administer the frontier as it existed, not to create a new frontier and begin all over again on the old plan". Under this new treaty, in 1851, Chief Maquoma became a Chief Magistrate for the British Government.

In the five decades of military fortification in the area of Colonial settlement, much heart searching was done to justify what action was taken against the black Africans living in the Kat valley. Dr Philip wrote to the London Missionary Society:

> "I wish it to be understood that I do not object to the extension of the colonial boundary to the Kei River provided the lands are secured to the *Caffres* as has been the case in all our conquests in India. It is to the extermination of the *Caffres* that I object"

A lone, but unattended, voice of Lord Glenelg, Colonial Secretary (1835-1839) ventured his opinion:

> "In the conduct which was pursued towards the Kaffir Nation by the colonists and public authorities of the Colony through a long series of years, the Kaffirs had an ample justification of the war into which they rushed with such imprudence at the close of last year... The claim of sovereignty over the new Province bounded by the Keiskama and the Kei must be renounced – the original justice is on the side of the conquered."

A poignant end to Maquoma's life came in 1853 when he died at the age of 75 on Robben Island, still a political prisoner.

Important in Afrikaans history is the event of The Great Trek which occurred over a period between 1836 and 1838. This had far-reaching effects for South Africa, and ostensibly put the Dutch settlers at odds with the English for many years afterwards.

It occurred as a result of a groundswell of feeling on the part of the Dutch-speaking colonialists and in direct response to policy changes made by the British Government and the British Governor in the Cape. Whereas Xhosa chiefs always regarded any lull in aggression from the European colonists as temporary, the Dutch settlers had come to see that cheap labour and security with plentiful and accessible land were an essential part of their future existence.

In 1838 the treaty with the Xhosa in British Kafferia having broken down, the territory between the Fish River and the Keiskama River became a district of the Cape Colony with the name of Victoria East. This was the start of the separation of South Africa into independent States as the Trek had displaced 10 000 from the Cape Colony and dispersed the Boer farmers into many different regions of the country.

In fact the British Government became very ambivalent with regard to the problems created for them by the settlers. In 1852 Earl Grey, as Colonial Secretary wrote:

> "Apart from the very limited extent of territory required for the security of the Cape of Good Hope as a naval station, the British Commonwealth and Nation have no interest whatever in maintaining any territorial dominion."

The Xhosa tribes surrendered finally to Sir George Cathcart, forfeiting some of their tribal lands, and brought to an end the costly frontier wars. The policy of white settlement which followed was responsible for a "chequerboard of small white and black squares" which were created in the area which later became the Ciskei and the Transkei.

It is worth mentioning a sad and, almost fatal, self-harming action on the part of the Xhosa in 1857. This became known as the "cattle killing event". Chief Kreli, from beyond the Kei River, used the prophecy of a spirit medium to persuade the tribesmen that, if all their cattle and crops were destroyed before the 18th February of that year, their ancestors would protect them in an attack against the European settlers. The tribes responded in an act of supreme superstitious fervour around the area east of the Kei River. The famine which followed, and the enormous death toll amongst the Xhosa communities, opened up more areas for European settlement and the white population increased from approximately 1 000 to 6 000.

Many new settlers arrived from the German Legion that had fought with the British. Fort Peddie was where my grandfather, Robert, was born. His father was said to have originated from Germany. My mother has described her Grandfather Petzer as having a 'military bearing' so he was probably brought to the area as a young child by his family who arrived with the military forces in 1856. The German-British Army had engaged together in the Crimea and many were commended for their bravery. At the end of the War young German officers, seeking exciting new opportunities, travelled to England, then accepted overseas postings, with their families, in the new colony in the Cape.

This added to the increasingly diverse mix of European origin in the region and a healthy growth of infrastructure with schools and hospitals to meet the needs of the rising numbers of white settlers. Greys Hospital in King Williams Town was founded at this time. In 1860 a Crown Colony constitution giving control of East London under a Lieutenant-Governor was granted. Through assisted immigration, 12 000 new immigrants from Europe arrived in the Colony.

In 1865 British Kaffraria was annexed to the Cape Colony with two representatives in the House of Assembly and the following year the Cape Government assumed direct control of the Ciskei. However, in 1872 there came the introduction of Responsible Government in the Cape Colony and a federal ministry included representation from East and West Kaffraria. This was altered in 1874 when a Legislative Council consisting of 21 members, 7 for each of the provinces, were elected for seven years.

Still troubled by errant tribes in 1879, the Cape Parliament passed the Peace Preservation Act and, to try and instil British authority and frontier defence, the British Flag was hoisted at the mouth of the Umzimvubu River at Port St John's. A direct reaction to growing Dutch resentment was the birth of the Afrikaner Bond. Founded by Rev S.J. du Toit, what became known as 'The Bond' was intended to protect the interests of Dutch-speaking farmers and encourage the use of Afrikaans as a language.

Interesting events in South African history were The Convention of London in 1884, when the possible independence of the Republic of Transvaal was discussed, as well as a new pass system which "allowed the Bantu freedom of movement". In 1890, Cecil John Rhodes became Prime Minister of the Cape Colony. In support of his race policy he wrote:

> "There should be equal rights for all civilised men south of the Zambezi (e.g. one who has sufficient education to write his name and is not a loafer)".

Which philosophy shortly opened the way for franchise qualifications to be imposed to prevent 'blanket Kaffirs' of the Transkei territories from obtaining the vote. In 1894 the Glen Grey Act applied in the District of Ciskei, encouraged Bantu to own land on European tenure and establish District Councils of their own.

In 1898 the Afrikaner Bond won an election and W.P. Schreiner, Cape Advocate, became Prime Minister of the Cape Colony and there followed two momentous events for my family. On 25th December 1899 my grandmother, Hester Aletta Coetzer was born, in the same year that the Anglo-Boer War began, and in January 1900, the year that Lord Roberts handed over command to his Chief of Staff, Lord Kitchener, my grandfather, Robert Peter Petzer was born. (Robert always complained that he had married an 'older woman'.)

Chapter 2

By all accounts Hester grew into a lovely young woman. She had bright-blue eyes, flaxen hair and was strong and healthy. Born an only child to Katrina Elizabeta she was her mother's pride and joy. Katrina was a member of the Bezeitenot family, of French Huguenot origin, which owned farming land in Balfour in what had recently become the Ciskei. True to Africana tradition whereby land was divided between all the children born within a family, Hester stood to inherit a farm from her mother. In fact the Roman Dutch Law of Inheritance had ended in the Cape Colony in 1874 as it had perpetuated an unsustainable division of property amongst all the sons in each family. This had resulted in inherited farms becoming smaller and smaller. It had also created a trend of intermarriage amongst farming communities and the law had been repealed in an effort to restore the viability of farming in the region. It is clear, however, that the Dutch communities in the Eastern Cape sought to maintain the policy of keeping land within families and Katrina's siblings also maintained farms in the Balfour region.

Hester was given the very best of everything as she grew up. She was well educated and learnt to play the piano. Speaking high Dutch, she had an appearance which bore testimony to her ancestors which were the original Javanese Dutch settlers who had arrived in South Africa during the Napoleonic Wars. A deeply analytical mind led her towards the profession of bookkeeping, and she was much sought after by small businesses in the neighbouring towns to manage their accounts and one of her cousins from a neighbouring farm, a young boy at the time, remembered her riding to work in a horse and cart. It was an image which he remembered until the end of his life.

In fact, young Afrikaans girls were encouraged to marry Afrikaans boys in order keep the land within the Dutch speaking community and Hester was lined up to marry a young man called Jan Els whose family owned a nearby farm. This is where conflict grew between mother and daughter because when Hester met Robert she became totally smitten by him. Robert did not suit any of the requirements as a match for Hester as far as Katrina was concerned. He was one of ten children, did not stand to inherit any money or land, and worst of all, his family were English-speaking.

Robert was very tall, good looking and had sparkling brown eyes. The cheeky smile which lit up his face would have melted the heart of anyone who met him, anyone that is except Katrina. She didn't approve of him and put up a strong opposition to his developing romance with Hester. If the truth be told, Robert was a bit of a rogue and often caused mayhem in and around the town with his friends on their frequent drinking binges. His habit of challenging authority got him into many scrapes throughout his life, but as a young man he was charmingly outrageous. This endeared him to Hester and she would not look at any of the farming boys, much to the frustration of her mother.

In the end Hester got her way. She was a strong-headed young woman and having made her choice stuck by it and eventually Katrina relented. In fact, approaching 22 years old, Hester was quite late to marry by Afrikaans standards. It is likely that Katrina saw that her daughter was getting older and was less likely to make a good match. In her view it would have been essential that Hester found a man to marry who would protect her. With the turmoil that the settlers had become used to over the years, it was unthinkable that Hester would remain unwed. In the end, Robert would have to do and the young couple were married in 1921.

Hester often related an amusing story of her wedding night when she sat in the nuptial bed awaiting the arrival of her new husband. Robert entered the bedroom and began slowly to disrobe. His wife stifled her giggles as he divested his body of clothing and stood naked before her, wearing only his hat. This he solemnly took off and put it carefully and lovingly aside before he joined his young wife in the bed. Robert always wore a hat.

The birth of a baby boy, Frank, followed in October 1923 and the young family settled in nearby Seymour. At that time transport between the small towns was usually undertaken by horse-drawn trap, but Katrina always walked the journey, between Balfour and Seymour, on a weekly basis, accompanied by two small black girls carrying bundles of vegetables on their heads. The produce was grown on the farm, although the main crops in the area were citrus fruits and tobacco.

It is a point of interest that many of the original Dutch speaking farming families had actually left the Eastern Cape area in 1838 having joined and become part of The Great Trek. The fact that the Bezeitenot descendants had not gone with them raises certain questions. The reason could have been that they were very comfortable with their situation and had no reason to seek change, or perhaps they didn't agree with the reasons behind the mass exodus of the Dutch settlers.

The changing frontier policy from 1835 onwards triggered discontent amongst Cape Boers. No security of tenure had been given to white farmers and this resulted in poor farming practices. They had become a race of extreme individualists with an inherited suspicion of authority and discipline. Where the British government was intent on maintaining a fair and equitable way of dealing with black Africans, the abolishment of slavery had devastating consequences for those depending upon free labour on the land. At the start of Louis Trigart's Trek in 1835, farms were sold or abandoned and men were willing to uproot their families and subject them to an uncertain future. The dangers from tribesmen in the interior and the physical hardship caused by rough terrain did not dissuade them. They hitched their covered waggons onto spans of oxen and followed what seemed to be a collective reaction. In fact the trek-spirit was inborn in these people. Many of them had descended from small scale stock farmers and huntsmen with experience of hardship deep within their history. A poorer standard of living did not result in such a great change in their way of life.

A second Trek under Andries Hendrik Potgeiter was undertaken in 1836. This went further east where the Highveld land could support livestock and corn crops. The result of this Trek ended in near disaster when, having been granted the use of a vast area of land by Makoena, Chief of a small clan of the Basuto Nation in the area of the Vet and Vaal Rivers, the Trekkers were swarmed by a Matabele horde, their waggons surrounded and food and cattle stolen. In retaliation, an expedition of Boers attacked Matabele kraals nearby and killed 400 people and drove off 7000 head of cattle. This resulted in the formation of a Council of War with Potgeiter as commandant.

Famous trekker Piet Retief in his Grahamstown manifesto written in 1837 tells of feelings of injustice towards the British Government and distrust of the missionaries who had opposed the stand against stock thieves in the Cape region which led to deprivation and loss to the farming community. Very telling words came from his niece, Anna Steenkamp, who wrote:

> "....the shameful and unjust proceedings with reference to the freedom of our slaves; and yet it is not so much their freedom which drove us to such lengths, as their being placed on an equal footing with Christians, contrary to the laws of God, and the natural distinction of race and colour, so that it was intolerable for any decent Christian to bow down beneath such a yoke; wherefore we rather withdrew in order thus to preserve our doctrines in purity."

In fact the Dutch Reform Church gave no blessing to the Trekkers and instead gave its support to the South African government of the day, whose members were British. After the Trek the Church became split and two sects were created after disagreement amongst the members.

Seymour was home to a very harmonious white community and provided a happy environment for the growing Petzer family. Within the small town the tobacco factory was a prominent building sitting on a crossroad in the vicinity of a street which passed as a shopping area. One shop was owned by a Jewish family which served all the practical requirements of the community stocking everything from foodstuffs to gifts and toys. Robert worked as a chauffeur for the man who was in charge of a fleet of vehicles run by the tobacco factory. He had a gift for fixing cars and could diagnose problems with a motor from the sounds of the engine. He always had a vehicle to drive, usually a Chevy.

Into this setting, on 30th November 1926, a second child was born. This time a daughter, Catherine Elizabeth, named after her maternal grandmother, but shortly afterwards her name was, for some reason, changed to Kathleen. In this year the Government created the Nationality and Flag Bill when two separate flags were adopted. Henceforth Union Nationals were to be British subjects and thus Kathleen was entitled to be a British citizen. A report presented at the time defined Dominion as:

> "Autonomous communities within the British Empire, equal in status, in no way subordinate to one another in any aspect of their domestic or external affairs, though

united by a common allegiance to the
Crown and freely associated as members
of the British Commonwealth of Nations."

Hester's mother, Katrina died, quite suddenly, six months later, probably as a result of an infected gall bladder which has been a recurring inherited weakness amongst the women of the family. Upon her death Hester inherited the farm in Balfour.

Kathleen was a bright and caring little girl. She developed a strong relationship with her 'Oupa', Martinus Johannes Coetzer, who came to live with the family after the death of his wife, and he absolutely adored her. He did not inherit any part of the farm and had not gained much wealth. The old man could not speak any English at all, only speaking Afrikaans, but he had memories going back to the first Anglo-Boer war of 1880 when he had been a small boy, probably aged about 10. He told the child stories of leading ox waggons carrying supplies for the Boer fighters giving her a sense of her own cultural identity. He was a gentle and gracious, non-drinking, man and was however completely at odds with his son-in-law, Robert, who treated him badly and was often sarcastic towards him. Robert may have found him a bit soft as he did not behave in the 'drinking, fighting and hell-raising' way that was regarded as 'manly'. In any event, he suffered extreme poverty in his life after leaving the farm in Balfour and was probably the victim of a syndrome of low achievement which had dogged Afrikaners as a direct result of the Great Trek.

The educational backwardness in the frontier districts in the 19th century became a cause for concern for the government. The roaming habits of the Boer settlers had developed in them an ability to survive under hardship as well as giving them inherent farming skills. But education of the children suffered, and this set up for the future, what became known as, the 'poor white' problem in the country.

In 1933 it was reported to the new Fusion Government formed by Hertzog of the Nationalist Party and Smuts of the South Africa Party, that due to extreme economic hardship, one fifth of Europeans within the Cape could be classified as 'Poor White'. The definition of this was given by the Carnegie Commission as "someone of European descent who could not support himself according to even a moderate European standard of civilisation". In the rural areas 30% of the European population lived precariously on the land as 'bywoners' or squatters.

Not much is known about the fate of 'Oupa' Coetzer. He returned to Alice, when he left Seymour, which was where he had originated and also had been the birthplace of Hester. At the age of 64 he became a general gardener working for the Municipality.

Chapter 3

The political climate during this time caused more and more disadvantage to black South Africans. In 1921 the Pact government of Hertzog and Smuts had embarked on a course to try and disguise the poor white problem by giving preference to Whites in the allocation of unskilled jobs, mainly in the railways which was a huge employer of lower-paid workers. In 1926 the Colour Bar Bill closed many avenues for Bantu and Asians to obtain work. Domestic employment became the main income generator for many black African families and the economic distinction between the races started to become evident with their dependency on the more prosperous Whites. Hester was a generous-hearted employer and had a good understanding of the tribal customs of the Xhosa people who lived nearby. Quite often she was asked for help when a mother arrived at her door carrying a sick child and she would give advice and whatever she had in the way of medicine. As a result she was greatly respected, and even loved, by the local Blacks and they might bring her a gift, such as a goat led by a tether to her door, or perhaps a live chicken, by way of grateful payment for restoring the health of a child.

Kathleen was aged 18 months when her brother John was born in June 1928. The black *Aya* (maid) who lived with them and was regarded as part of the family acted as midwife. Both Kathleen and John were delivered at home assisted by *Aya*, who was also the Nannie and maid. Hester spoke the Xhosa language fluently and maintained a close domestic relationship with the *Aya*. They worked side-by-side in the kitchen and around the home. The *Aya* had total authority over the children and their respect for her was unaffected by any racial differences.

Kathleen learned very quickly that she needed to be quite wily to negotiate her own way in life. She was up against a strong mother, a bigger brother and a tough maid who stood no nonsense.

Kathleen's Anecdote 1:

Trip to the Cinema

A visit to the cinema was a regular family outing from Seymour to the bigger town of Fort Beaufort. Robert's Chevy truck was usually fully loaded on these trips and the Aya was included amongst the passengers. She was never able to watch the film because Blacks were not permitted into this cinema. She usually stayed in the truck to look after Kathleen who, aged 2, was too young for the 'bioscope' (movie theatre).

On one such occasion, upon arriving at the cinema in Fort Beaufort, Robert probably parked amongst other Chevrolet trucks. This was a popular make of vehicle in South Africa in 1928. The parking area was a patch of rough ground outside the entrance to the building.

The family, which included Frank, aged 5, spilled out of the truck and made their way towards the cinema. There was a

Charlie Chaplin film showing. The billboard outside promised that they would all be laughing helplessly as this was a very funny film. Kathleen watched in dismay as her loved-ones walked away leaving her in the dark car park with the Aya.

The truck cover had been pulled up to provide shelter and the Aya settled down comfortably in the back as Kathleen scowled with resentment. This was not much fun for her.

After a short period of quiet contemplation the child spoke up.

"Aya, I need to pee" she announced with a desperate expression on her face.

The maid, feeling lazy and not wanting to shift from her comfortable position said "Ok, just go down there next to the door," and pointed down towards the stony ground beneath the vehicle.

Kathleen jumped down onto the ground. The Aya could not see her in the dark and was completely unaware when she sneaked away from the truck and scampered across the car park towards the cinema, guided by the bright lights in the doorway.

Finding that the entrance hall was deserted, the little girl followed the sounds which led her towards where the film was playing. It was a silent movie and she could hear a piano and hilarious laughter coming from within. The promise of humour was obviously fulfilled because the audience were enjoying the film a great deal. Their mirth was loud and prolonged and came intriguingly from within the cinema.

Unnoticed Kathleen made her way through the double doors and stared with astonishment at the chaotic performance which was underway on the large screen ahead. There was a strangely dressed man with a moustache and bowler-hat leaping around obviously in huge distress. He occasionally fell down with uncontrolled and jerking movements, but then jumped up again, running around in his effort to escape some disaster. Then Kathleen saw why he was so upset. He had somehow managed to get a small animal stuck inside his baggy trousers, and the long tail could be seen emerging from the opening at the front. All the while the audience was laughing wildly, and unsympathetically, at his misfortune.

All this was too much for Kathleen and she started to cry loudly, the tears streaming down her face. The Aya, having noticed her disappearance, had followed her inside. Fortunately, because of the loud laughter, she had not yet been noticed by anyone within the room and the maid quickly scooped her up and carried her outside, back to the safety of the Chevy.

While being severely scolded by the angry Aya, Kathleen felt that nothing that happened in her life could ever be as bad as what was happening to that poor man in the bioscope.

Hester and Robert enjoyed a very communal lifestyle in Seymour. Members of both families including aunts, uncles and cousins were very much part of their lives. Hester's cousin Sarah married her cousin Willem and they lived nearby.

The community, comprising of about 50 homes, was largely English, with an English doctor, Dr McCarthy, and the Anglican Church had a vicar with a long white beard call Rev. Stumbles. Robert was not a religious man, but if he did attend church it was the Anglican Church. Hester, on the other hand was very much involved with the Dutch Reform Church and played the organ there on Sundays. Religious tolerance existed because Hester would also occasionally play the piano at the Anglican Church.

A number of Jewish families lived in Seymour and in the house opposite her own lived Kathleen's friend Miriam Obromowitz whose father owned the local store. Jews were regarded with great suspicion by the, increasingly powerful, right-wing element of the Nationalist party as many had arrived from Russia and brought with them the taint of Communism. This was identified as a peril which could inflame the uncertain climate surrounding Company Unions and black workers. The thinking of the Government was to try and exclude whites from organisations which included black and coloured workers and Jewish employees were suspected of organising 'Kaffirs' as their comrades. This attitude towards Communism escalated over the years and in 1939 Charles Harris, a Jew and the Secretary of the Mineworker's Union, was assassinated by a young Afrikaner who believed he was a Communist taking orders from Russia

Robert had attended the same school as Kathleen subsequently did and had lived in Seymour most of his life, but his father, when he died in 1929, had been living in Alice in the Eastern Cape. Robert's mother died when he was a young boy, and his father was said to have married for a second time which may have complicated family relationships. In any event, when the old man died the Petzer family travelled the long and tedious journey to attend his funeral.

Kathleen's Anecdote 2:

Stolen Pennies

It was approximately 60 km to Alice from Seymour. The year was 1929 and Kathleen was 3 years old. Robert's father had, in his later years, lived near Alice and the Petzer family travelled to attend the funeral.

It took them two days in the old truck, travelling over rough terrain, and they finally arrived at the homestead which was already filled with family members, most of whom lived some distance away and hadn't seen each other for many years. Sad though they felt, the adults had a lot to talk about and there was a rather festive air about the occasion. Food had been laid out on a large table inside the house and on the front porch the men stood together drinking beer.

Robert and his family were shown into the room where the body of Grandpa Petzer was displayed in an open coffin. Robert had not seen his father for some time and was moved to see the old man lying there so peacefully.

Frank was just tall enough to look over the edge of the coffin and Kathleen was lifted by her mother in order to let her see her grandfather. It immediately registered with the little girl that the old man had pennies placed over his eyes. They were English pennies, with the head of King George showing prominently on the face of the corpse.

Eventually the family left the room together and joined other guests who had come to the house to pay their respects. Murmurs of sympathy could be heard as they acknowledged the end of the life of a good man. No one noticed Kathleen creeping back into the room where her grandfather lay. She hitched herself up on a chair placed next to the coffin and with dexterous little fingers removed the pennies from his eyes. She pocketed the coins and left the room.

A short while later there were sounds of shocked exclamations as the news travelled from person to person that the pennies had been stolen. Hester looked around and scrutinised the small form of her daughter who was, at that moment, straining to reach some food on the buffet table. The little girl was the thief, much to everyone's amusement.

Kathleen was allowed to keep the pennies and the memory stayed with her for the rest of her life

In Seymour, at that time, some children were exposed to the disease of meningitis which was endemic amongst the black Africans living in the reservation some way out of town. Hester lost two children to this disease following the birth of John. There was a little boy called Bobby, who unfortunately died at the age of 14 months, and shortly afterwards baby Emma who, aged 5 months, died of the same disease. This must have caused enormous grief to Hester. Kathleen remembered that, aged 4 she helped to carry the coffins at the funeral of her siblings. The ceremony was led by the Dominie of the Dutch Reform Church and six little girls carried the coffins to the 'Whites-only' cemetery where the babies were buried. Twenty-five years later these graves were drowned when a Dam was built and the water from the Kat River engulfed the grave yard.

Chapter 4

Hester was a businesswoman by nature. It offended her sense of worth to be unproductive and she was actively involved in bringing money into the household. At that time Robert was in employment, but he often drank his wages away before Hester managed to get hold of them. She ran a sixteen-roomed boarding house mainly serving the men who worked on the railways nearby. When the weekends arrived, the young workers arrived on the train for a Saturday night dance, and then they would stay overnight. Hester had a special friend; godmother to Kathleen, whom she called Auntie Bapes. She was the adopted daughter of the local doctor. Together the two young women prepared for the Saturday dances by making dresses on Hester's sewing machine. They copied the fashions of the 1920s from magazines and added beadwork, a craft done by local white girls. When the dancing began Kathleen would remain hidden as she watched everyone enjoying themselves with her mother playing the piano. The women looked very glamorous as they danced around, kicking up their legs, the tassels on their dresses swirling around. The little girl loved to see Hester looking so classy and felt very proud of her.

Hester was very much involved with the Afrikaans community through the Dutch Reform Church. During the flu epidemic in 1918, local women involved with the

DRC had provided soup to the sick and dying in the area, and she always maintained a strong identity with her cultural roots. Hester spoke Afrikaans in the home, even though Robert only ever spoke English, and as Kathleen grew up she was proficient in both languages.

The lovely hills and valleys surrounding the Kat River gave a sense of peace in a land tormented by political strife. The Church helped to bond those who farmed the area. Frequently the Afrikaans families would eat together down beside the river where they could swim in the lazy waters. On one occasion a large water-monitor lizard (Legavane) emerged from the depths onto the bank. Everyone panicked and ran screaming from the river thinking it was a crocodile. But there were no crocodiles in those waters.

Sometimes the families abandoned their homes during the hot weather and travelled further afield. Kathleen remembered that for about a month, each year in the summer, large numbers of Afrikaners gathered at St John's in the Eastern Cape. As many as twenty families camped together on the beach. They would sleep under shelters, eat the fish that they caught and play Boer-sports. The children played on the warm sand while the women pickled some of the fish that the men caught and packed it away ready to take back to their homes at the end of the holiday. Robert would have been working and only arrived on the beach to join the family occasionally.

Kathleen never understood the vicious arguments which her parents often engaged in during her young life. She knew that, during his drinking binges, her father was likely to become steeped in resentment and anger. She knew too that he was intensely jealous of the men that Hester had known in the past and this became the focus of his resentment. "I am not a man's arse" he would announce heralding an unreasonable rage which sometimes resulted in Kathleen and her mother hiding under the stairs while her father rampaged around the house, sometimes wielding a gun for effect.

As she matured Kathleen realised that her presence had a calming effect on her father's moods. Though she was never able to stop his drinking bouts, the pretty young girl used her powers to best effect and learned how to manage the menfolk in her life. She had become her mother's ally and friend. Afrikaans culture recognizes a matriarchal status for women, but men are very much elevated on the basis of gender alone. Afrikaans women in a family will attend to the needs of the males before those of the females and serve their food first at table. In time, Frank, as the eldest son, would be deferred to in the same way and Kathleen was often expected to give way to her brother.

Daughters were often brought up to observe these customs. Hester never challenged Robert's behaviour in any way and endured physical and verbal abuse without complaint.

Normal family life had its ups and downs. The three children, though generally healthy, had normal childhood ailments and injuries which Hester usually attended to with her special remedies. However, after a period of persistent throat infections it was decided by Dr McCarthy that Frank needed to have his tonsils removed.

Kathleen's Anecdote 3:

Frank's Tonsils

Kathleen recalled an occasion when Frank, aged 5, needed to have his tonsils out and the event offered her an amusing interlude in an otherwise boring day. Frank had been primed for the experience and promised a toy car if he was a good boy.

This promise was in fact, the one thing that caused him to hesitate. Why would he need a bribe? What was so awful that he should get a present, but the others wouldn't? It was a bit of a puzzle, but not worrying enough to stop him accepting the offer. The toy car that he wanted was red. He had seen it in one of the shops in Fort Beaufort where they often looked, but seldom bought, any of the exciting products imported from abroad.

The journey was short in their old Chevy, Robert driving with Hester beside him and in the back were Frank with Kathleen and baby John. At the last minute, a couple of the neighbours' children joined them, leaping into the back of the truck as it drove away. They were keen to see what would happen to Frank during his forthcoming ordeal.

On arriving at the home of the Doctor, the group, trouping through the door, was shown into the kitchen by his smiling wife. The kitchen table had been especially prepared with a clean white cloth and the Doctor's instruments were on display. Frank viewed these with huge dismay – this was getting serious. There were tweezers, small, sharp knives and most disturbing of all, a spoon-shaped utensil which looked as if it might have an important function in the procedure.

38

"Hop up young man" said the doctor nodding towards the table as he gave his hands a good wash in the kitchen sink.

Frank obediently climbed up and lay down on the table. Without giving him too much time for doubt, the doctor dripped some ether on to a mask which covered his nose and mouth. This was an accepted form of anesthesia at that time and the patient was, without doubt, completely comatose throughout the operation.

Adults and children alike looked on with fascination as the tonsillectomy was performed by the family doctor. The spoon-shaped instrument was used to good effect when two bloody tonsils were scooped out and placed on to a little tray. The children were all very quiet, their eyes wide with grim interest.

When it was all over and Frank had emerged from his stupor, he was helped down from the table and carried out of the house into the Chevy. Realising that he was now in some pain, he started to sob and it was clear to Hester that the small boy needed a quick diversion. Instead of going straight home, they went to the shops and Frank pointed to his prize which was on display in the shop window.

Later on, back at the house, the children looked on in envy as Frank, all on his own without sharing, played happily with his new red car. Any pain that he had felt seemed to be forgotten.

Kathleen started school in Seymour aged 4. She was very bright and always top of the class in Sub A. When she was 5 years old she started Sub B at the farm school in Balfour when the family moved from Seymour. Hester had sold the farm in Balfour and bought a garage situated at the crossroads from East London to Queenstown, where a rough road descended from the Hogsback. This was primarily for Robert's benefit and it was, potentially, a lucrative business. The garage had a workshop, where Robert mended cars, and also sold petrol. Hester did the books and they lived in a house behind the garage premises.

Sad to say the garage went out of business, despite Hester's careful handling of the accounts. Robert was not a good businessman; he enjoyed doing favours for people and never insisted on receiving payment for a job before it was finished. He liked to keep on good terms with customers and his nickname was 'Happy', which says much for the way he dealt with those who owed him money. The problems encountered were not totally down to his poor judgement. In the early 1930s South Africa had entered the gold standard which put many people out of business during a resulting recession and devaluation of the currency. When it was sold the business was heavily in debt and creditors had not been paid. A rich Indian man bought it and the family moved into a house in Balfour.

In fact very few Indians lived in the Cape choosing instead to settle in the Natal area. However, the influence of Gandhi in 1931 had caused the Immigration Laws which discriminated against Asians to be repealed and restored the rights of those Indians born in the Cape Province. The Indian man who recognised the potential of the rather worn down and dilapidated garage in the heart of the Eastern Cape certainly had every right to conduct a business in that region. He probably followed the trend of others of his race and managed to turn it around, financially, in a very short time.

Hester got a job as an accountant and the family moved into a thatched house which had two mud-built rondavels at each end with the living-quarters between the bedroom areas and a surrounding veranda. The floors were in the African style of compressed cow dung, which was a very efficient and hard type of flooring. A small generator provided electricity.

Chapter 5

S chooling in Balfour, for Kathleen, was linked to the farming community, with farms all around and most of the children attending the school from farming families. Pupils were transported to and from school in a lorry. Kathleen often played with the neighbouring children who worryingly sometimes built tunnels inside haystacks.

During the years that the family lived in Balfour, the surrounding farms were, from time to time, threatened by hungry locusts. Warnings of the approach of swarms were broadcast over the radio and regarded with such seriousness that all the children in the area, both black and white, were taken out of their classrooms or homes and sent into the nearby wheat fields where the crops were in grave danger of being devoured by these insects. Each child was given a tin can and a stick. They all walked around the fields creating a cacophony of sound that must have been deafening. This was done before the locusts managed to land in the hope that the swarm would be deterred and move on to some other farmer's land.

The Bezeitenot family owned a farm near Kathleen's school. The farmhouse was built on stilts, probably to deter snakes from going inside. A flight of wooden steps led up to the front porch. The farm produced a citrus crop and had quince hedges surrounding the orange groves.

Delicious quince jam was sold locally, and the ripe oranges were taken to market at harvest time. Sometimes Kathleen would hide in amongst the orange trees and eat the fruit because she really loved oranges. The farm grew vegetables and kept livestock for their own purposes and on Sundays the whole family got together for lunch at the farmhouse. Hester would play the piano while everyone stood around singing hymns, even Robert enjoyed the singing, even if the words were in Afrikaans.

In fact members of the family, in the name of 'Nel', still maintained the farm into the 1960s, long after other white farmers in the area had left, when it was renamed 'Transkei'.

Kathleen would long remember very happy times in Balfour. When she was six years old her little sister, Dawn, was born in June 1932.

Kathleen's Anecdote 4:

Fetkoeks on the Road

They set out before dawn. The truck, prepared by Robert, was ready for a long dusty journey to East London. The four children, Frank the oldest, 9 years old, Kathleen 6, John, two years younger and the baby, Dawn, were all were bundled sleepily into the Chevy. They had been coaxed from their beds and loaded along with provisions and, uncomplaining because this was the norm for them, they snuggled comfortably together, squirming and huddled together like puppies on the back seat.

As they drove along the dusty highway, southeast towards the sea, the sun made her appearance above the mountain range to their left spreading the pink mantle she wore over the African plain. Shadows of the sparse trees shortened as the day arrived. Insects, lively and glad that the cold night was over, ended their lives with a splat against the clean windscreen. That was just the start, by the end of their journey the glass would be covered with bloody smears.

Kathleen poked her head up over John's sleeping form. "I feel hungry Ma" she announced. Hester smiled and nodded as if confirming to herself what was expected. It was always Kathleen who got hungry first. Like baby birds in a nest they all waited for their beaks to be filled, but Kathleen always opened hers the widest.

Their father, eyes on the straight dust strip ahead had managed to coax the old engine into a pleasing rhythm. He knew that this was the best time to travel, while it was still cool before the sun rose higher.

"Rob, we should stop for breakfast" said Hester hoping that her firm tone would not irritate her husband. He was surely hungry and would not mind a break in their journey.

Reluctantly Robert brought the old Chevy lovingly to a stop at the edge of the tar strip. Already the heat had made its effect and the water had started bubbling inside the radiator. He opened the bonnet to allow a breeze to cool the engine.

Hester went round to the back of the truck and opened the hatch. She dragged out the old, black, three legged pot and several baskets and boxes. In the meantime, Frank, Kathleen and John knowing the routine, walked into the scrubland beside the road looking for pieces of wood. They came back each laden with good, dry, twigs and Hester, after scraping a small hollow in the ground, set a fire.

Before long the fire had taken hold, the poikki *(iron pot) stood firmly over it and the fat placed inside was starting to sizzle and melt. In the meantime Hester, sitting on her haunches, was kneading small lumps of dough in her hands. The children watched as she plopped each little blob into the bubbling fat and hooked them out with a spoon as they started to turn brown. She piled them all onto a tin plate, one at a time.*

This was their breakfast. Fetkoeks *(donuts) eaten hot with honey drizzled over them in the morning of a new African day. The family sat eating by the roadside until they were full. Not another person could be seen.*

Robert, having failed to run the garage as a successful business was, nonetheless, an excellent mechanic. His reputation alone brought him work and he could be relied upon to fix a car engine, if it was humanly possible, and sometimes he would seem to perform a small miracle. On one occasion he was called upon to do an emergency job. A man, travelling on the rough road from George, brought his vehicle to Robert with a leaking petrol tank. A sharp stone had made a hole underneath and the fuel was seeping away.

Robert spent many hours of that day, and into the night, welding the tank and making it safe to drive. In fact, he did such an excellent job that the man, who was extremely grateful, told Robert that he would give him a job if he ever came to George. So, with amazing spontaneity, which gives evidence of how desperate their situation had become, the family packed up and moved to George.

As it turned out, the man was a director of the Forestry Commission, and he gave Robert a job as the foreman in charge of a fleet of lorries used to haul logs from the stinkwood forests. In fact logging in the Cape forests was well established in 1933, and the communities of woodcutters who settled there were of English origin. Robert, as an English-speaker, was very much at home with his new employment and had, definitely, fallen on his feet. On this occasion his open-hearted and sociable nature had served him well.

Hester travelled, with the children, to George from Balfour on the train. Kathleen, aged 7, was two years above the age of free travel. She spent the whole journey huddled under a blanket beneath the seat, hiding from the ticket collector, because Hester didn't want to pay for her ticket. John was two years younger than her, and Dawn was still a baby, so they were exempt from payment. Only Frank, aged 10, had his ticket paid for. Kathleen's resentment towards her elder brother started to build in her young mind as she crouched uncomfortably on the floor of the rattling train. The railway track took many turns up the mountain towards George.

The family moved into a nice house in George which is situated at the foot of the Outeniqua Mountains that lie parallel to the coast. It was named after George Rex, the son of the English king, George III, in 1802. The town had wide roads with luxurious vegetation surrounding large houses in uniform style. Large gardens were packed with agapanthus and hops which were strung up and tied onto eucalyptus poles. Hester had brought the *Aya* with them and she was very proud of the lovely new home not letting the children play inside during the day unless their mother was there.

Hester would often take the children up into the mountains during long summer days when they went picking Cape gooseberries, *roiboos* tea and big bunches of wild flowers. In the early morning the small group would climb up the green slopes as the mist crept down the mountains and into the pine forest and dark gorges. Outeniqua is a Hottentot name meaning "honey-laden men" from a time when local tribesmen collected honey in the heaths.

Robert worked every day for the Forestry Commission, and earned a decent wage, but they were still quite poor and always seeking ways to earn a little extra money. Coming from a farming family, it was natural for Hester to grow vegetables in the garden, and they never went hungry.

Kathleen's Anecdote 5:

Lettuces

Kathleen at 7 years old was great friends with Hester. She was the eldest daughter and enjoyed the privilege of being an important part of her mother's world.

One morning, sitting cross-legged on the large bed that her mother shared with Robert, Kathleen watched Hester getting dressed with a critical eye. She had seen pictures of pretty women in magazines and loved to study their fashionable clothes and the way they wore their hair in modern styles. Her mother, by comparison, looked drab and ordinary as she put on her day dress in front of the mirror.

"Ma, why don't you wear nice dresses in bright colours?" she asked. "That one looks about ready for cleaning cloths!"

Hester looked around towards her daughter. "When do I ever have money to spend on clothes?" she asked. "I have too many hungry mouths to feed. There is no money left for such things."

Kathleen, now thoughtful, slid off the bed and went out into the yard. The lettuces in the vegetable garden were plump and ready to be picked. She knew that they were intended for the family to eat but, after a slight hesitation, the little girl made a decision and pulled out, from the shed, a large carton. One by one, she pulled the lettuces out of the ground and placed them into the cardboard box.

Where they lived in George was not far from the centre, and Kathleen walked with her precious crop into the town. Once there she set the lettuces out on display beside a shop doorway. Although very young, she nonetheless understood that people who were walking past were probably doing some shopping. It was likely that the area in front of a window display might draw attention to her from people who had money to spend.

The window she had chosen was a dress shop, and the clothes on display were of the kind that she would have liked her mother to wear. The white mannequin dummies gazed down at her. Elegantly static, they seemed to focus on the unlikely *sight of the small girl setting out her wares on the dusty road outside the shop.*

Kathleen did not charge much for her lettuces and she sold them all quite quickly. The coins, slipped into her pocket, felt heavy and, as far as she was concerned, must be worth a lot. Her customers must have thought it was strange to be buying from a young child and one woman was curious enough to ask why she was selling these lettuces.

"I would like to buy my mother a pretty dress" she replied with disarming honesty.

The lady was taken aback for a moment. "What a very special thing to do!" she declared. "Your mummy is very lucky to have a caring daughter like you".

Kathleen was a bright child and had always done well at the farm school in Balfour where she had a special friend called Elaine Dempsey. Her parents, being quite well off, planned to send their daughter, an only child, to Outeniqua High which was a very good boarding school. Elaine's mother and father were very keen that Kathleen should be allowed to go to the same school to keep their daughter company. They offered to pay the cost of her books and board at the school and this would have been a great opportunity for Kathleen, but Hester refused to let her go. She could not bear to let Kathleen go away, and wanted her to stay at home.

Chapter 6

A very patriotic English community in George had built a small Roman Catholic cathedral where a statue of St George, dressed in khaki as a soldier, stood in a memorial window. Kathleen passed the entrance exam and was accepted to attend the Convent school where the teaching standard was very good. Inspectors visited regularly to test each subject taught at the school and it was run by nuns of the Roman Catholic Church. The dress code was very strict and this sometimes caused problems for Hester. The nuns required that the girls' gymslips always reached a certain level above the knee and would regularly check the length. Kathleen was growing fast and soon needed a new uniform which Hester could not afford to buy, so she lengthened the entire dress by adding material at the shoulders. But despite these efforts, it was difficult to comply with the high standards set by the Mother Superior at the convent. Kathleen was often sent back home with a note for her mother. The distance to and from the school was quite far for a small girl and she was wearing uncomfortable shoes handed down to her from her brother Frank. She would slowly make her way along the road, wasting most of the day. Dawdling to and from school in this way must have taken up a lot of learning time for Kathleen. When she finally arrived home, with the note, Hester would invariably write a terse reply and send her straight back to school again.

Poverty was a stigma at the Convent where some pupils paid fees and others, like Kathleen, were there on a charitable basis. Hester, knowing that a clean, white, handkerchief was a requirement as part of the uniform, would collect the hankies given free with 'Joko' tea, and gave her one of these to carry in her pocket each day. This, and the fact that Hester actually sewed a straw hat on to her fair hair, to stop her removing it, before she set out for school in the hot sun, brought Kathleen unwelcome attention and she, and her mother, were regarded as intractable by the pious nuns.

Kathleen's Anecdote 6:

The Loquat Orchard

One day Kathleen was walking in the grounds of the convent with some of her classmates when they came across a loquat orchard next to the garden of Father Meaker. The six girls peered over the fence and could see that the fruit was nicely ripening; indeed some loquats had fallen onto the ground and would be wasted if someone didn't pick them up very quickly.

Kathleen, taking a leader's role, and guided as usual by her stomach, went to the door of the house, and when the priest opened it, asked in a strident tone.

"Father Meaker, if those loquats can be spared, please may we pick some to eat?"

"Of course my child" said the priest, a beatific expression on his face as he looked down at the girls.

With his permission the children walked purposefully into the orchard and filled their bags and pockets with as many ripe loquats as they could carry.

Later that day, during a sewing class, Sister Carmelita walked into the room.

"Will the girls who picked the loquats in Father Meaker's orchard please raise their hands?" she said.

All six girls lifted their hands innocently unaware of the consequences.

"Please follow me" said the nun and led the little girls into the lobby, single file. There they were to be properly punished, as the Good Lord required, for their thieving ways. A good spanking with the back of a hairbrush was what God would want, and Sister Carmelita was to be the one to undertake this painful duty.

Kathleen, as the leader, was placed in the front of the line and was the first to have her bottom soundly smacked. Then she was sent to the back of the queue and after the punishment had been administered to each of her friends, she had her bottom smacked again.

The unfair treatment she had received was very bewildering and at the end of the day Kathleen again went past the house of Father Meaker. He was standing in his garden looking at her from the other side of the fence, still wearing the same beatific expression. The man of God did not discuss the matter with the small girl but just turned and walked away towards the nearby cathedral building where he was due to perform mass.

In 1933 Hertzog and Smuts formed the Fusion Government with six Nationalist members and six members of the South African Party. In 1914, as a result of a rift in the Union Cabinet, Hertzog and his supporters had launched the new Nationalist Party to represent the interests of Dutch-speaking South Africans and introduce compulsory mother-tongue education. Then in 1934 the Nationalist Party under Dr D.F. Malam formed a purified Nationalist Party which became the official opposition.

The Afrikaans language had historically been under siege in South Africa since 1822 when the Somerset policy of anglicising education resulted in rural, Dutch-speaking, parents keeping their children away from school. A further setback had occurred after the Boer War in 1902 when Lord Milner had put a stop to the use of the language within public services and schools, and banned all Afrikaans newspapers, in an effort to quell dissent from the *Broederbond* (Fraternity).

A 'dual medium system' under the new Government was proposed by Jan Smuts whereby all children would be taught in their mother tongue and learn the other as a second language in the classroom. It was felt that everyone would benefit from this new policy as children could be educated in the language that they were most familiar with, but would mix with and make friends with other children, using each language, outside the classroom but in the same school. Speaking each other's languages would bring about a better understanding of the two cultures, and the strife that had been enflamed through political differences over decades, would be eased by a new generation of children starting within their school environment.

Kathleen benefited from this new system at the Convent because she was from a bilingual home and spoke both languages equally well. She chose to attend general classes in English with Afrikaans as a second language. This resulted in her doing very well in her Afrikaans classes and she was always top of the class.

There can be no doubt that this school had a strong bias towards English-speaking pupils and deference was given to the British monarchy. In 1937 all the children at the school were grandly presented with a commemorative mug to mark the coronation of King George VI.

The Convent education, though difficult at times, served Kathleen well. She had gone into Standard 3 when she first started at the school, and aged 10 went up to Standard 4.

In 1938 a Voortrekker wagon party, travelling from Cape Town, passed through George and camped there for a while along their journey. Children and adults of the town joined them amongst their covered wagons for a *braii* (barbeque) and Kathleen went along and joined in with the festivities. They wore the original Trekker costumes; the women in long dresses over petticoats and wearing poke bonnets as their forebears had done one hundred years previously. This was the Anniversary Trek which started in August 1938 at the Jan van Riebeck statue in Adderley Street in Cape Town and their destination was Pretoria. Two wagons named 'The Piet Retief' and 'The Andries Pretorius' were used and the route was set to visit towns and villages along the way.

The history of this event had begun when Dingane, King of the Zulu nation, signed his cross, before witnesses on to a Treaty over land ownership with Piet Retief in February 1838. However, in an act of huge betrayal the Zulus attacked and murdered Retief and his followers where they were camped nearby. In fact the Zulu chief had become alarmed as huge numbers of Trekkers; close to 1000 wagons, were assembling in the Natal region with an expectation that they would be able to settle in the area. There followed a massacre of the Boer families at Weenen and 40 men, 50 women and over 180 children perished together with some 200 Hottentot servants. Thousands of sheep and cattle were driven off by the attacking tribesmen.

On 15th December 1838, a platoon of 500 Boers, under the command of Andries Pretorius, struck a force of ten thousand Zulu *Impis* along the banks of the Ncome River. Taking them by surprise in the night they slaughtered 3000 tribesmen with guns. Thereafter this became known as the Battle of Blood River.

The Hertzog Government gave strong backing to the Anniversary Trek and planned to build a monument to commemorate the Battle of Blood River on its hundredth year anniversary, 16th December 1938, named by the *Broederbond* as *Die Dag vad die Verbond* (The Day of the Covenant).

Huge passions were aroused amongst Afrikaners in response to this occasion as this was regarded as a sacred pilgrimage. It took on an enormous significance and was linked in the minds of the Afrikaans people with a sense of national pride. New Afrikaans names were given to streets in towns along the way and recognition of the Afrikaner national anthem *'Die Stem van Suid Afrika'* (The Voice of South Africa) was given. A new respect for their language was sought. Along the way the Dominies of the Dutch Reform Church organised reception committees and relays of oxen were provided for the Trekkers.

When they arrived in Pretoria, the foundation stone of the new monument was laid on the *Monumentkoppie* (Monument Hill). Each year following the Anniversary Trek, Afrikaners have assembled in Pretoria, on the Day of the Covenant, to lay wreaths and stones at the Voortrekker Monument whilst reciting the vow to reaffirm a united *Broederbond*.

It interesting to note that, although the young Kathleen was present at the celebrations held in George by the Anniversary Trekkers, none of the adult members of her family joined her. It is likely that many Afrikaners did not agree with the principles encompassed within the vision of this occasion. In fact the Great Trek itself had fostered many of the deeply entrenched problems which the Afrikaans-speaking people were now experiencing. There was evidence that there was educational backwardness within the outlying Cape districts dating back to the 19th century and the Boers had not achieved social development to the same extent as settlers in Australia and the American Midwest had. This could be directly attributed to the lack of schools and learning available to the children of Afrikaners. The 'poor white' problem was a great anxiety for the Government and Dr Malan, a Dominie of the Dutch Reformed Church, had a fear of whites living alongside non-whites, and of European children "growing up like kaffirs".

The encroachment of the Trekkers on to tribal land had created a landless class of Bantu who then became squatters, and the problem did not ease with time as there was an increase in the divisions created by the lack of farming land. In 1910 Blacks could still purchase land and, in fact, in the Cape could still vote on the common voters roll. However, in 1913 Louis Botha brought in the Native Land Act which set aside areas for native reserves. The British Government had never thought it prudent or necessary to set land apart for occupation by native Africans.

In 1936 Barry Hertzog, from within the dual Government, took Blacks off the common voter's roll with the Representation of Natives Act, but made more land available to them with the Native Trust and Land Act passed in the same year.

The Boers, with their extreme form of nationalism, had set a trend of ignoring any requirements of any other culture within South Africa in the interest of furthering White-only interests.

Where the Eastern Cape was concerned, the original Great Trek had displaced over ten thousand Dutch-speaking farmers from the Colony when they travelled into the interior. As a result the whole of South Africa was broken up into several independent states. This was the start of a great and abiding animosity between the British and the Dutch.

Chapter 7

A t this point it seems apt to introduce a person whose life started and ended in the Eastern Cape. He was born on 18th July 1918 in the small Xhosa village of Mveso which sits on the Mbhashe River, a little to the east of the Kei River. His name was Rolihlahla, which means 'troublemaker' in the Xhosa language, but he is known to the world as Nelson Madiba Mandela.

Madiba was his clan name earned through his royal lineage as the great-grandson of the King of the Thembu people whose homeland lay deep within the Transkei territory, a gigantic area the size of Holland, which stretched north to the border of Natal. His grandfather, Mandela, had been born to a lesser wife of the King and thus was unable to attain royal status, but gained prestige within the tribe as a councillor to the King. Nelson Mandela's father, Gadla Henry Mphakanyiswa, became a local chief in 1915 when the existing chief was convicted of corruption by the governing white magistrate. Gadla had four wives, as his station allowed, and each lived in a different village. Nelson's mother, Nosekeni Fanny, was his third wife who lived, with her children, in a village called Qunu. In a typical Xhosa kraal, she maintained three huts and kept cattle, sheep, goats and horses which grazed together in a common pasture.

Living in a kraal was a very communal existence with just a few hundred people sharing a common area. Mud-structured huts were beehive shaped, built around a single wooden pole and with a thatched roof. The floor was made from the fine earth from an ant heap and smeared with cow dung to keep it hard and smooth. Often the huts were distinguished by a unique design which was painted on the outside. Viewing a village from a distance, one would see a rural African scene with women in traditional costume, water jugs balanced on their heads, carrying babies, wrapped in shawls on their backs. They all worked together within the kraal and children tended the animals in the fields. Nelson took on responsibilities for herding cattle at the age of five, along with other boys in the village. Long hot days in the *veldt* (fields) were spent in this way and when a car drove along a road nearby the children from the village would pelt down the hillside in their droves to wave and run alongside the vehicle. The sight of black, healthy, children along the roadside was a common part of travelling through the African plains. Hester, packing the Chevy for a trip would bear in mind the little *picininis* (black children), big-eyed and naked, whom they may encounter on their journey and she always carried some sweeties to hand out to them. Perhaps it is possible that a member of the Petzer family once placed some tasty thing into the grasping hand of the young Madiba, before driving off in a cloud of dust.

Nelson as a young boy was only superficially aware of White people. Those who travelled in cars and ran shops were White, but nothing in his early life required him to give much attention to the significance of colour. Tradition and superstition had a huge influence over his world where the lapses causing dishonour to ancestors could result in ill-fortune unless atonement was sought from the village elders. Mandela would later learn that his whole existence as a black South African was guided by political men, of a different colour and culture to his, who lived very far away.

Since the Native Land Act in 1913 black Africans could not own land in the Cape, but were tenants who paid rent to the Government. After the Glen Grey Act of 1894, Blacks were encouraged to farm land on British tenure within reserve areas and maintain administration through District Councils. Since that time the Xhosa territories had become subject to a game of political chequers which brought constant uncertainty and poverty to the Xhosa in their tribal homelands. Family groups were unsustainable where people could only eat what they produced themselves, and usually villages were inhabited by women and children only. Overstocking of cattle and poor agricultural practice had created huge cracks and *dongas* (gullies) in the soil and the land was exhausted by overpopulation. The menfolk had to travel far to obtain work, either in the gold mines of the Transvaal to the northeast or within the white-owned farms as workers, only returning to their kraal for short periods for the harvesting of crops.

The value of education was recognised by the Methodist Missionary Society formed in 1932. This organisation had established churches throughout Africa especially benefiting those living in rural areas. Nelson was sent to a local school run by the Methodist Wesley mission. His father was not a Christian, as his spiritual beliefs embraced the rituals of his tribe. However his young son went proudly off to the one-roomed Methodist schoolhouse on the other side of the hill, wearing a pair of his father's trousers tied at the waist with string. It was customary for children attending mission schools to be given an English name which may or may not be habitually used. The teacher bestowed upon him the name of 'Nelson', and he chose to keep it, even though it is doubtful that he knew much about the culture from whence it originated. In a strange way the lives of the young Nelson and the young Kathleen were running a parallel course. Both were given names at birth which were changed early in their childhood. They both attended Christian schools where the bias upon British culture was evident, and these establishments gave each of them a good educational grounding. Both children developed a deep love of the same beautiful Cape Province countryside, and lived within the same region, but with huge cultural differences.

In repayment for a past favour on the part of Mphakanyiswa (Nelson's father) the regent of the Thembu people, Chief Jongintaba Dalindyebo, took over guardianship of Nelson upon the death of his father. He lived in the royal household which comprised two western-style houses with tin roofs surrounded by *rondavels* (mud huts). The schoolhouse was within the compound and the royal children were taught from English books whilst writing on black slate. The Methodist mission station, Mqhekezweni, was run in the style of the early missionaries and the women wore long skirts, high-necked blouses and scarves wrapped around the head like a turban. The somewhat austere environment may have got a rebellious response from the young Nelson.

**Anecdote from *Long Walk to Freedom*
by Nelson Mandela:**

Stolen Mealies

The little boy stood dismayed at the edge of a fenced area. How was this possible? There were mealies growing inside that place; dozens of ripe mealies. They were standing-up proudly; their tassels waving in the wind indicated that they were ready to be picked. Did nobody want them?

The crop was in the garden of the Reverend Matyolo who lived in a nearby hut with his wife. Nelson did not really understand the idea of a garden. Where he had lived in Qunu with his mother, everyone grew their maize in the fields, but there was never any need to put a fence around the plants. Everybody in the village grew crops for their families and when the mealies were due for harvest, everyone knew which were theirs to pick.

The young boy remembered how he had plucked the ripe cobs and carried them in a blanket to his mother's cooking hut. She would tip them into a large, wooden grinding bowl ready to be pounded into maize-meal. As a reward he could take for himself, one, or maybe two, yellow mealies to be roasted over the kitchen fire.

As Nelson stood watching the ripe maize in front of him, he understood that the flimsy barrier which surrounded them was not a serious attempt to prevent theft. In fact a little push could have destroyed the fence. The message being given by the Reverend Matyolo was that this was a symbol of separation which excluded others from the delicious treat within his garden.

Scooting himself up onto the edge of a wooden post, the African child reached out and took as many cobs as he could hold and scampered off to hide in the bush with his prize. With expert hands he lit a fire and laid the mealies in the flames, turning them over and over until they were brown. He ate hungrily and with great enjoyment then made his way back to the hut he shared with his cousins.

When Sunday came the members of the church assembled underneath a tree and the glorious sound of harmonious singing filled the air. The Reverend Matyolo stood in his robes to give a lusty sermon and the congregation were enthralled. Nelson stood, smartly dressed, within the crowd as the holy man stood back and his wife stepped forward.

"This boy has been stealing the food which was provided by our Lord", the woman pointed towards the boy as he cringed away.

The Regent's wife continued to rant and vicious words were rained down on the small thief. Young as he was, Nelson was keenly aware that the public nature of this rebuke brought great disgrace to him and his family.

"The devil may seek to bring punishment down upon you!" was the threat thrown at him by the woman, now made hoarse by the force of her anger. "You are the vile manifestation of a soul that has lost the protection of our Almighty God".

The young Madiba eventually shook himself free of the fear created by the superstitions of his people. Time would reveal whether or not harsh retribution followed because he took some mealies from a garden.

According to Xhosa tradition Nelson achieved manhood at the age of 16. This involved a rite-of-passage circumcision and spending a month alone within the African bush. This event was an annual occurrence in all villages when young men who had reached the appropriate age attended an "Ukutshila" dance, covered in white clay and wearing a headdress and tunic. The young initiates or "Abakwethas" could often be seen during the following weeks, maybe at the roadside and distinctive in their traditional garb, ghostly at night when caught in the headlights of a car.

Mandela started his secondary education at the Clarkebury Boarding Institute in Engcobo, which was the largest school for black Africans in Thembuland. This was a colonial-style building where shiny floors and an impressive staircase presented a precarious problem of slipping to a young man unused to wearing shoes. Nelson received the type of education intended to prepare him in for a future as a counsellor to the Regent's son, Sabata.

In 1937 when Kathleen at the age of 11 was a pupil at the Convent School in George, Nelson aged 19 went to Healdtown Methodist College in Fort Beaufort. As a member of Thembu royalty he was introduced to a life of relative privilege in comparison to other young men, whether black or white, within that region. However, Mandela would later reflect that the education received at Healdtown was biased towards an English view on life with pupils encouraged to believe that the British were superior in every way. But, if he gained anything during that time, it was a deep feeling of kinship with his fellow black Africans, and more particularly the Xhosa tribe.

The life of Nelson Mandela is well documented and it is of interest within the context of the Petzer family history that he started his university education in Alice where Hester was born and Robert's Father lived for the latter part of his life. The original Fort Hare, built in 1846 was part of a string of fortifications constructed by the British Army as part of the frontier war defences against the marauding Xhosa warriors. Alice was an important town in the Eastern Cape being the seat of magistracy, later known as Victoria District. In fact Fort Thompson had been constructed as part of the Mfengu settlement protection programme as there was rivalry between the Xhosa and Mfengu clans. Historically the Mfengu had arrived in the Eastern Cape fleeing from the Chaka Zulus as refugees in 1840. A passive tribal attribution meant that they were willing to work on white farms and within European businesses and thus were looked down-upon by the proud warriors of the Xhosa. Over time the Mfengu developed educationally and being industrious were able to become teachers, clerks and policemen in the community. They became Christians and so enjoyed the protection of the British against any resulting jealous attacks from the Xhosa. In 1853 the German ancestors of Grandfather Petzer arrived as part of a contingent stationed in Alice as part of the protection programme after the Crimean war when elite officers were invited to follow careers in the British army. They were encouraged to marry whilst they were in England and often arrived in South Africa with English wives.

Fort Hare was established as a university for Africans in 1916 by Scottish missionaries. Mandela attended as an elite student being groomed for success and was hard working in his studies towards being a translator in the

Native Affairs Department and a civil servant. It was here in 1940 that Nelson Madiba Mandela developed a taste for politics having become a student representative on a Council which hitherto had been unsupported by the student body. He encouraged a boycott of the elections for student representation and was expelled as a result of insubordination against the Council.

A poignant thought that springs to mind is that Mandela, along with other students from the Fort Hare University, sometimes walked into Alice town and ordered food at a restaurant there. As Blacks they were served outside, behind the kitchens. The Petzer family might well have been eating inside that restaurant at the same time.

Chapter 8

Fortune smiled on Robert in his job at the Forestry Commission. He was very adept at maintaining the fleet of trucks and in 1938 was given a promotion and the family moved to Knysna on the coast. The ancient and natural woodland was densely primeval with trees dating back to 246AD. Yellowwood trees grew to enormous heights and Stinkwood and Oak edged the forest where wild elephants roamed freely.

Robert was now a foreman in charge of the entire logging operation; a position of trust and prestige. He earned sufficient money for the family to live well and they moved into a large house in Long Street. The home was situated on a sizeable plot and Hester with her usual financial prudence kept and bred pigs. Kathleen took a great interest in the benefits that the pigs might bring to the family and collected acorns daily as a treat which the pigs must have enjoyed. In fact they must have been very happy to see the young girl arriving with her skirt laden with their favourite morsel, and probably rushed towards her as pigs will do in their rather high-handed way. This trust was surely misguided because Kathleen only ever saw pigs, or any other animal for that matter, as being ultimately useful. On one occasion the industrious young girl scooped up one of the piglets, whilst its mother was occupied with acorns, and before it was missed, carried it away. She took it to a nearby hotel and, entering the kitchen offered it for sale. Seeing a tender sucking-pig as an attractive meal option for his guests, the manager gladly agreed a price and Kathleen took the money home to her mother.

Not long after they had arrived in Knysna, Hester gave birth to a little girl and in August 1938 Kathleen had another little sister called Cynthia.

Life was good for the family and Hester was happy with their new prosperity, but she was always connected in a very fundamental way with the culture of the black Africans. She spoke their language fluently and, while this may have been for somewhat paternalistic reasons of communication with farm workers in her youth, she nonetheless felt a kinship with the people of colour who shared her world. She had an understanding of the local tribal customs and a deeply-felt respect for their superstitions.

Kathleen's Anecdote 7:

The Fortune Teller

"I think it's this way" shouted Dawn, aged 6, running ahead on a forest path.

Hester, with baby Cynthia on her hip, walked alongside Kathleen. They were looking for the hut belonging to the Fortune Teller. Having recently moved to Knysna, the area was still a little strange to them.

When they came across a small shack in amongst the trees they knew they had arrived. It was evident that the lady who came out to greet them didn't usually entertain visitors. She was a Coloured woman, of uncertain age, very thin with no front teeth. Standing amongst a variety of livestock which ran around the yard, she studied the approaching group with sharp, black, eyes. Hester introduced herself, and her daughters, explaining why they had come and they were ushered into the wooden homestead.

Before going inside, Kathleen released the scrawny chicken that they had brought by way of payment and watched as the other hens immediately started to attack the stranger. This unfortunate bird would undoubtedly be used during some disturbing ceremony in the future. It was better not to think about it. Not for the first time she was left bemused at the rather pagan tendencies of her mother and wondered what the nuns at her convent would have said if they could see her now.

She followed the others into the hut where they had all settled down on some chairs around a table. The fortune teller spoke to each in turn in rather loud, chanting, Afrikaans. She seemed hardly to draw breath as she held forth, but at one point lifted her body sideways and farted loudly without pausing. Kathleen fought to keep a straight face as her fortune was being told.

"You will travel over the water", declared the crone. "You will marry a man dressed in blue with shiny buttons". This information seemed so specific that Kathleen felt inclined to think that some particular explanation was necessary, but none was forthcoming and the woman only gazed at her with a bland expression in response to her questions.

They took their leave and Hester placed a few coins on the table as an extra payment; after all, the chicken may not have been noticed and it would be unwise to invite a curse.

As they were walking back the way they had come, they discussed what the fortune teller had said.

"I wonder what the 'man in blue with shiny buttons' will be" said Kathleen hoping that her mother could shed some light on the puzzling words.

"It sounds like it might be someone dressed like a clown" answered Hester helpfully, although she had secretly hoped that her daughter might marry a rich farmer. "Maybe it will be a man who works in a circus".

Kathleen conjured up a mental image of herself, in the future, walking down the church-aisle on her father's arm. Ahead of her, waiting to receive his bride in all her finery, was her husband sporting a red nose and big painted mouth. Perhaps he would be holding a bunch of exploding paper flowers and precariously riding a small, one-wheeled, cycle. She imagined the look of astonishment on the faces of the guests and the disapproval of the waiting priest.

Kathleen started to giggle. Hester joined in and so did Dawn. The woods echoed with the sound of their laughter as they wiped the tears from their eyes.

"Well, he might be a very kind man", said Hester reassuringly. "He will definitely be amusing."

Kathleen was skipping in the street outside her home when someone called out to her that a World War had begun and South Africa would be a part of it. Her response was ambivalent as one might expect from a 12 year-old girl. Her interest was held only by those things that affected her directly. She had grown aware that the political changes within the country in which she lived did not usually impact upon her, or her family.

In fact the occasion of South Africa joining the European war had very great significance. The Fusion Government headed by General Herman Hertzog of the Nationalist Party and General Jan Smuts of the South African Party, each with six members, were very much at odds as the reality of the War became apparent. Hertzog as the Premier wanted to keep the Union of South Africa separate and neutral from the events in Europe. It was a time when the Nationalist Party very much desired independence from Britain and Germany had offered assistance towards this end. In the event, after the matter was put to the vote Hertzog was defeated by 80 to 67 in Parliament. This caused a break-up of the alliance between the two Parties and General Smuts was free to form a new Government made up only of his own party. On the 5th September 1939 the Union and Germany were at war.

But the sun continued to shine in Knysna with its beautiful headland and gentle climate. Not for long however. Clouds were gathering for the Petzer family as Robert became more complacent about his responsibilities towards his family, and his drinking became heavier.

One day he had been travelling along the road outside the precincts of the town and had inexplicably parked his truck on the wrong side of the road. This was, and still is, against the law in South Africa and Robert, sitting inside his vehicle, drew the attention of a party of policemen who had been attending a football match in Knysna. It is not unlikely that these policemen had been drinking alcohol themselves. However having conducted a search of Robert's Chevy and discovered a bottle of whisky, they took him into custody.

The disposition of the South African constabulary was never a gentle one, and their happenchance finding of Robert in such a situation was something of a disaster for him. The police force was made up mostly of a certain type of rugged Afrikaner, and Robert had a hatred of the Dutch which ran very deep. He always refused to speak Afrikaans, even to Hester who found English difficult. On this occasion, and being much the worse for having consumed best part of a bottle of spirits, he was undoubtedly very antagonistic indeed.

The four policemen placed themselves on the wrong side of the law when they took Robert, by car, to their own area of jurisdiction, which was George, and there he was charged and found guilty by a magistrate. Given the option of a R50 fine or 3 months in jail he agreed to pay the fine and returned to Knysna to give Hester the devastating news.

Hester was, by now, used to dealing with catastrophic change and immediately approached a local shop manager for a loan to pay the fine which was due immediately. Then, in order to pay back the loan, she sold Robert's car.

He was, naturally, incensed by this and declared that he would rather spend three months in jail than lose his car, but Hester insisted. Possibly in her mind a man who had fathered five children was not entitled to the luxury of languishing in prison.

As things turned out, the white man who bought Robert's car didn't pay the agreed price. He paid a portion of it and nothing else was forthcoming. Several times Kathleen and John went to his house which was five miles away along the river. He was married to a black woman and lived as a recluse in the forest. When the two children begged him to pay what was still owed he simply said that he didn't have any money to give them.

The Director of the Forestry Commission heard about the incident, but was unsympathetic and the outcome of Robert's behaviour was that he lost his job as foreman.

Kathleen's Anecdote 8:

A Visit to the Witchdoctor

Who knows what caused it? Dawn had always been an anxious child with a sensitive nature. Now, at the age of 6 it seemed that her normal childhood moods had turned into something more worrying. She was often found lying on the ground, staring ahead of her, seemingly in a trance-like state. Once or twice she had been found lying rigid, jaw clenched and legs stretched out. She seemed to be having fits.

Kathleen knew that her mother was worried, but a visit to the local doctor would cost money. Robert was out of work again and Hester was finding it hard to hold things together. She had lost two children some years before to meningitis, a disease which had been endemic amongst Africans at the time.

Kathleen had seen her mother crying, and praying to herself "Please God, not another. Please!" This seemed to initiate a decision which led them to visit the local African healer.

They set off on foot. Kathleen aged 12, her mother and Dawn, being led by the hand, entered the Location area, which was the land set aside for black Africans, and walked into the African kraal. There was an area of hard-packed mud surrounded by thatched rondavel-style mud huts. African women walked around, relaxed and at home in their environment. Children played in the dirt. All stopped to stare at the small group of white people entering their domain. It was a rare and interesting sight.

Hester spoke the tribal language fluently and had a brief exchange with one of the women. She was directed to a hut on the outskirts of the village. This was where the 'Witchdoctor' lived.

They approached the entrance of the hut cautiously and Hester knocked on the dilapidated wooden door which hung on makeshift hinges. They were summoned into the dark hut by a masculine voice and stood huddled together as their eyes became adjusted to the gloom.

An elderly black man sat inside the hut on a low stool. He was wearing nothing but a small, frayed, apron which covered his private parts. Beads adorned his neck and arms and he had a headdress made of various types of feathers. On the floor in front of him were the tools of his craft which comprised numerous animal bones and various wooden and plastic items. This was the village healer, an important man commanding huge respect.

It was customary to assume a position below a man of high status, and Hester quickly ushered the girls to sit on the floor in the middle of the hut. The old man listened intently, as she explained the nature of the problem, and he nodded sagely at some points. When he had heard all she had to say, he struggled to his feet and with a rather bow-legged gait, walked over to an area of the hut where various bottles, containing a murky liquid stood in a row. In a bowl he made up a potion which he poured into a bottle and gave to Hester.

As they walked home, they studied the contents of the clear, unmarked, bottle. It seemed to be the colour and consistency of egg-nog. Kathleen felt glad that she would not be the one to use this medicine which needed to be smeared over Dawn's body. How much Dawn benefited from this treatment was never clear, but in time her health improved and she did stop having fits.

The Katburg near Seymour from the Hogsback 1930

Robert and Hester with Kathleen, Bobby
and Emma in Seymour 1930

Chapter 9

Robert failed to get another job and things were beginning to look desperate. He made the decision to leave Knysna and go to Herald in search of employment.

Herald was situated on a very rough road up in the mountains between Outzhourn and George where Robert felt that his skills as a car mechanic would be more in demand, unlucky travellers being more likely to seek urgent maintenance in such a remote place.

Hester was left behind to pack up the house and she joined him, together with the children, a few months later. When they departed Knysna their furniture and possessions were stacked precariously on to a lorry and the family travelled in the cab. Unfortunately, there was no room for Kathleen inside and she sat in a chair, which was secured with rope, on top of the pile for the entire journey. They travelled all night and into the next day along a mountain road which was winding and dangerous. This route climbs high through lush green forest where yellow, peaty waterfalls create pools in the rocks. At the top the countryside becomes a different type of terrain, more like a desert with scrubland where small succulent plants survive in sandy spaces. Aloes and prickly pear cacti are silhouetted against the sky. This is a barren countryside where only goats and hardy sheep can survive. The contrast as they got further away from Oudshourn, where in the distance valleys lined with poplar trees could just be seen, was stark.

When the weary family arrived in Herald, the sun was already high in the sky. Kathleen slid down from her high perch and lay down by the side of the road not having slept all night. She awoke when a concerned woman passer-by urged her into the shade, fearful that she would burn her fair skin and get sunstroke.

In fact Herald was situated on what later became the Montague Pass and the town no longer exists. At that time when the Petzer family arrived in 1939 there was a fair-sized community living there with businesses, a school and a railway station. Kathleen had reached Standard 7 at her school in Knysna where only four children were English-speaking. She continued with her lessons in Herald and her bilingual home life gave her an advantage in Afrikaans classes, but she continued to learn other subjects in English.

Robert was able to obtain work as a mechanic in a garage but he left promptly when he discovered that the owner of the business was an 'OB'. This was a reference to the 'Ossewabrandwag' which was a group of extreme members of the *Broederbond* attached to the Nationalist Party who were engaged in anti-war activities even to the extent of violently attacking those who signed up for active service in North Africa. They labelled servicemen '*Rooi Luisies*' (Red Lice) due to the red flashes on their shoulder tabs. Demonstrations by the *Ossewabrandwag* became common as the war progressed and an elite group of '*Stormjaers*' (Storm troopers) was formed. They had emerged as a direct reaction to the Anniversary Trek in 1938.

The *Broederbond* had originally developed as a secret society in August 1921. By 1925 there were eight branches which grew to twenty-three by 1930. It was organised around an Executive Council where membership bodies could exist, independent of other branches. The Federation of Afrikaans Culture (FAK) was a public organisation but within it was 'The Bond'; an underground movement whose objective was to further the cause of the Afrikaner Nation, '*Volk*', as a separate culture with its own language. The British were hated to the point of obsession by some Afrikaners, this view having historical roots dating back to the Anglo Boer War in 1899.

Kathleen was poignantly aware of the crisis that gripped her family while her father was out of work. She knew the anxieties that beset her mother and the degenerate nature of her father's moods if he felt he was being made to feel 'less of a man'. She felt a strong responsibility to try and turn things around and to this end approached the owner of a garage and asked him if he could give her father a job. The man was a little surprised at this request from a young girl, but explained to her that it was necessary for him to meet the actual applicant himself. This was probably said with 'tongue in cheek'. However, Kathleen took it as an invitation which she duly relayed to Robert. He in turn responded, believing that a vacancy for a job existed, and went to see the garage owner. Whatever transpired in the way of an interview is not recorded, but Robert was given a job as a mechanic and the family moved into a house attached to the garage.

Family life returned to normal for a while. Hester built a Dutch oven in the garden and Kathleen kneaded the dough for her to make bread twice a week.

Kathleen's Anecdote 9:

Cave Paintings

Kathleen aged 13 and John aged 11, had been out since early morning. Sent out to fetch wood for the Dutch oven, they picked up stray branches when they found them. The children proceeded slowly, mainly because they were both wearing great big, black, laced shoes. These had been handed down to them from Frank, who always had his shoes bought new. Their progress would have been easier without the shoes but Hester had given them dire warning.

"If you walk in the bush without shoes, worms will crawl up into your feet"

Kathleen respected this wisdom, but every African picanini she had ever seen was bare-footed. "Do they all have worms in their feet?" she wondered.

As they ambled across the undulating plain, flying insects created shimmering clouds around them. They could hear chirrups and bird sounds, even the air itself seemed to hum. From time to time they would stop and create a small pile of dry twigs ready to collect on their way back home.

"Hey, ou sis (big sister), I can see your broekies (knickers) when you bend over like that" said John.

Kathleen giggled. She loved her little brother. He made her laugh; sometimes so much that she clutched her stomach, doubled-up with mirth. He had a cheeky smile and twinkling blue eyes.

Seeking shade towards the middle of the day the two blond children make their way towards a kopjie (hillock) which rose up as part of the range of hills between George and Outzhourn. When they reached the rocky outcrop John kicked off the clumsy shoes and started to climb. His thin, strong legs stretched across the large granite boulders, and his agile feet sought cracks which supported his toes as he edged to the top of the hill. Kathleen looked up, eyes squinting against the sun. She was used to John taking off like an errant monkey.

When he reached the top, the boy disappeared and Kathleen sat down on a warm rock. After a while she heard a shout.

"Hey, ou sis I have found something up here. Come up, I will help you."

Kathleen kicked off her shoes and hitched her dress into her pants. Her passage over the rocks was slower than her brother's but eventually she arrived at the top and dusted herself down.

John was excited. "Kom op! (Come on!)" he said as he showed her the way through openings between the large rocks. Sometimes the passageways were so deep that they became like caves, then the light would find them again as they emerged.

Eventually, along the flat wall, on one side of a huge slab of granite, they came across some images. Mystical in the half light, were images of men, painted in a red colour. The artist had depicted human forms on rocks deep in the heart of an uninhabitable place. What had he wanted to say? Why were they there? The two children did not even stop to wonder. This was part of a culture that was not theirs to examine. They went on their way and gave it no further thought.

Note: These rock paintings are now a tourist attraction, and there is a Winery nearby which is called "The Red Man".

Hester became involved with the Dutch Reform Church in Herald and her social life was strongly steeped within the Afrikaans culture. The event of the *'Nachtmaal'* (literally 'Night Meal') was part of the calendar within any DRC community and was an event when members of the church took communion. Waggons would arrive from all the rural farms and outlying areas and form a circle within the grounds of the Church and all the babies that had been born within the previous year to members of the congregation would be christened at the same time over one weekend. Kathleen would become engaged with carrying the chubby babies to and from the church, and holding them while they waited their turn at the font. Wearing a panama hat to protect her from the searing sun, the young girl was always a willing participant in these lively parties when the *braii* (barbeque) would be lit and people would dance to the *Boeremusiek* (Boer music) played on an accordion. Robert never went to these gatherings as he never attended the Dutch Reform Church.

Having reached the age of thirteen, Kathleen stopped going to school and, responding to the family's financial need, went to work as an apple picker at a farm called Nomkloof. The job entailed stacking the fruit in such a way that they were firmly lodged inside a box. This was to prevent bruising caused by the apples jiggling about when in transit. It was Kathleen's first effort at gainful employment and she travelled dutifully to the farm each day. There was dormitory-style accommodation for the apple-pickers on the premises but Hester was adamant that her daughter return home after work. The women-workers were vulnerable to amorous advances on the part of the foreman, and Kathleen was still a little girl. She had no experience in fending off the unwelcome attention of men and she was very pretty indeed. Hester always kept a watchful eye on her daughter.

As it turned out the job did not last very long. Kathleen never managed to pack the apples in the correct way. The success of a packer was judged by whether the apples stayed inside the box when it was tipped on its side. Each time the foreman lifted the box that she had packed, the apples spilled out all over the ground and she repeatedly failed the test. Kathleen was paid-out for the short period of her engagement and then given the sack.

Chapter 10

At around this time Kathleen's relationship with her brother Frank began to deteriorate. She had always resented the special treatment that was given to him by Hester. In her view he had never made any effort to ease the financial trials of their family, and she thought he was spoilt and lazy. There were occasions when she felt bullied by him. One day, being required to kill one of their chickens, he forced Kathleen to hold the creature firmly on a log whilst he took an axe and chopped off its head. Much to Kathleen's horror the chicken then ran around the yard without its head, blood spurting from its neck. Frank, who must have known what would happen, found this hugely funny and laughed at his sister's dismay. The memory of the ugly incident kept her awake in the night for some time afterwards.

Now that her own puberty had arrived, she began to be aware of Frank as a young man with dubious tendencies. He was, after all, sixteen and showing a special interest in girls.

Kathleen's Anecdote 10:

Something Nasty in the Woodshed

Kathleen lay on her bed half asleep. In the house in Herald she had a bedroom to herself and enjoyed the privacy that it gave her. She was 13 years old. Her periods had started recently, much to her astonishment, and it was right for her to be separated from her brothers.

"You're a big girl now", her mother had said and showed her how to fold cloth napkins for protection. At the end of the spell of bleeding Kathleen had secretly made her way down to the river and, away from the sight of everyone, washed the bloody pads in the cold water and left them on the rocks to bleach in the sun. They would be stored until required again the following month.

As she relaxed on her bed enjoying the solitude, she became aware of a presence in the room. Sitting up quickly she saw Frank standing looking at her. "What are you doing in my room?" she shouted, shocked at the silent way he had appeared. He said nothing, just shrugged one shoulder.

Kathleen had certain knowledge about her brother which affected the way that she felt about him. She had recently come across him in the woodshed and was upset by what she had seen. Frank was inside the dark hut with the white girl who lived next door. They were probably enjoying some adolescent sex play and Kathleen was full of suspicion; the onset of puberty had brought about some disturbing changes in Frank's behaviour.

The fury over what she regarded as an invasion of her private space brought Kathleen to boiling point. She railed at her brother and accused him. "What do you want to look at me for? Are you thinking of sex with me?" Troubling fears came into her mind all at once. She felt strongly protective towards her younger sisters and feared that Dawn, and even Cynthia, would not be safe while Frank was around.

The noise brought Hester, moving with haste, into the room. She quickly summed up the situation. "What on earth is going on Kathleen? What are you saying to Frank? How can you behave in this way towards your older brother?"

It was clear to Kathleen that her mother would always support Frank against her. She would never listen to any of her daughter's complaints as she believed the eldest son deserved respect. Now, as Hester defended him, Frank removed his belt and offered it to her.

"Give her a good hiding Ma" he said. Kathleen knew that, as a female in an Afrikaans family, she would always be the loser in a battle against any of the men. This was a fundamental part of her culture, but one that she deeply resented.

Kathleen avoided a beating that day, mainly because Hester knew that her eldest daughter was a valuable ally against her husband when he became aggressive after a drinking bout. However, Kathleen never forgave her brother, Frank, and never trusted him again. Their relationship would always be tainted by the horrible memories that she held on to unrelentingly.

Frank was not a scholar and had only reached Standard 6 at school. Throughout his education he had positioned himself firmly with the Afrikaans-speakers, and was most comfortable with that language. When he left school his employment prospects were very poor and in Herald his future was limited. Robert's sister, Mary, arrived one day and took Frank to Grahamstown where he could live with her. It was hoped that opportunities would arise there which would enable him to develop skills, maybe as a mechanic like his father.

The departure of Frank must have been regarded with some considerable relief by Kathleen. However, shortly afterwards it was decided that the rest of the family would follow Frank to Grahamstown. The garage was not making any money and Robert was seldom required to repair any cars. People were more likely to break down in the desert area surrounding Oudzhourn which wasn't too far away. For this reason garages for vehicle maintenance had become a popular type of business in Oudzhourn and competition was strong.

The move to Grahamstown was an attractive one for everyone, even to Kathleen. This could be regarded as a small city with the Cathedral of St Michael and St George as the main church of Anglican denomination. The brown gothic building stood proudly at the center of a square in the middle of the town. It had been built by an architect called Sir Gilbert Scott and was cool and dark inside with a tall spire holding a bell-tower. Nave columns made of black Belgian marble were the pride and joy of the British congregation.

The town had wide streets lined by many shops with a department store called Bays and a ladies' dress shop called W.C. Gowie where all the clothes were imported from America. The Petzer family moved into a house in Beaufort Street. This was situated in a fairly central position a short walk from the market place. The house was of a typical colonial style; built of wood with a porch at the front. The roof was made of corrugated iron which made a deafening sound when it rained. Outside, at the back, was a dusty yard where Hester built her essential Dutch oven for the bread. The home was comfortable with a large kitchen where everyone could sit together and keep warm during the very cold winter months. There was a lounge which, though rarely used, was kept clean and tidy for special occasions.

Two doors away was a general store owned by a Jewish couple who had recently arrived from Russia. They were very happy when Hester came to work for them as most of the customers were Xhosa and she could speak their language. During her lifetime Hester had learned about the habits and purchasing requirements of the local Blacks. She would spend time making small skews of food commodities such as tea and sugar. The small paper packets containing just 1 oz were stacked on to the shelves and sold for 2p each. These were very cheap for the shop owners to make and customers would come in daily to spend their small wages, and then return again the next day to buy again.

The Africans who lived in the Black location area outside Grahamstown had absorbed the European culture and wore odds and ends of garments discarded by the White community. In the rural areas the Xhosa women wore the traditional costume of voluminous skirts and saffron-coloured blouses with turban-style head covering.

The Jewish shop keepers were part of an eclectic mix of immigrants who arrived in the Cape at that time. Many people fled Russia at the start of World War 2 with the threat of a German invasion and stories of the fate of Jewish people at the hands of the Nazis in Europe. Some Jews had found their way into South Africa which increased the anxiety of the Government about Russian communist involvement with the black work force. Whatever the political view of those Russians who settled in Grahamstown, no particular effect was felt by the existing White community which accepted them gladly and over time they prospered in Jewish-owned businesses.

Kathleen now turned fourteen and was happy to be living in a modern town where the women wore the latest fashions and there was more entertainment for young people. She still had her household chores and was expected to look after her younger siblings, but she was free to make some new friends and her life was full of light and laughter.

Kathleen's Anecdote 11:

Monkey in the Yard

It was 1940 and Cynthia had turned two years old. The 2nd World War had brought the British RAF forces to the region, car mechanics were in demand and businesses were thriving. Robert was usually fully engaged with fixing vehicles, and Frank was learning the intricate trade and developing the necessary skills for his own future.

No one knew quite where the monkey had come from. Frank had picked her up from the roadside when she was a baby. Her position in the dusty yard of the family home was unquestioned and the children generally left her alone. She had once bitten Cynthia who had innocently violated her territory in a fig tree in the back yard, and since then everyone gave her all the space she needed. She seemed to have accepted a fairly satisfactory truce between man and beast. No cuddles for her, she became a mean old lady

Her name was Hannah, now 'old Hannah' because she was getting on in age. She sat in her tree like an old African Aya contemplating her life. One of her arms was missing and it was likely that she had originally been rescued from a snare set by an African hoping to catch small game for the pot. Whoever it was might have been checking his traps and, coming across a baby monkey caught in the wire, chose to give it life so sold her at the edge of the road.

Snares in the bush were numerous and if any small animal was unlucky enough to step into one, the vicious wire would tighten as the animal struggled. The result would be painful with horrific damage to the entrapped limb. Perhaps Hannah had lost an arm as a result of such a snare, but had survived the encounter.

Her bright eyes observed all the coming and going, in and out of the yard. Always ready to fight for her place, she never demanded more than she was given. The result was a long life in a harsh land where people and animals fought hard to survive.

By 1940 there were close to 400 000 South African troops fighting abroad in the war. Under General Smuts there was no conscription, but women walked about the streets handing out white feathers to those who seemed to be avoiding their national obligation. At the same time, thousands of British Airmen were invited into the country which offered ideal climatic conditions for training purposes. The anti-war feeling of the Nationalist Party intensified and Hertzog and Havenga resigned their seats in the Assembly.

South Africans became aware that the *Broederbond* was actively engaged in sabotaging the war effort and providing espionage to Germany. One particular individual called Erik Holm, a former Natal headmaster, became a presenter on a German radio station and gave daily recitals of British atrocities suffered by the Afrikaners during the Anglo-Boer War. These broadcasts could be heard all over the world by anyone who owned a short-wave radio, and were intended to create despondency. One suspects that this man was regarded with some amusement by the general South African public as he was nicknamed 'Lord Hawhaw'.

In Grahamstown there was a camp for the Royal Air Force established a short distance from the centre of town. This brought about an intriguing new influx of young men into the community, especially interesting for the young women. These were known as the 'Brylcream Boys.'

Kathleen aged 15

PART TWO

PART TWO

Introduction to My Father

This is a glimpse into the life of someone I have always called "Daddy" who died at the age of 66, which at the time of writing is about my own age. I never did call him *'Dad'* or *'Father'* when speaking to him, even when I was grown myself with children of my own.

Grahame Knight Young was born 17th July 1921 to Charles and Dorothy Young who were living at that time with Dorothy's parents, Grandpa and Grandma Downey, at 39 Bellville Road, Clapham in London. He always joked that he was, in effect, a cockney having been born within the sound of Bow Bells. As an adult he actually had a pleasantly resonant voice with a rather refined accent and manner. He was born at the time of the Depression which followed the First World War when many families struggled financially. Grahame was the second child born to Charles and Dorothy, having an older sister, Enid, who was born in 1919. Audrey was born two years after him in 1923 and then two years later Marie who sadly died at the age of five. John and then Sibyl were the youngest in the family, close in age but eight and ten years younger than Grahame.

Grahame's childhood, he sometimes recollected, was not a particularly happy one. In his youth his father, Charles had contracted TB which affected his right leg causing him to walk with a slight limp. When I was a child I noticed his discomfort and stiffness, even when he was seated. He often seemed quietly brooding and had a pessimistic view of life. He did not approve of light entertainment on the radio, considering it to be "unadulterated tripe" as he reached for the radio's 'off switch' leaving any listeners in mid-chuckle. One fact I remember my father telling me was how his father reacted badly to the word "consumption", another name for TB; such was his fear of the disease which was rife in London. So it was a bitter blow that Audrey contracted TB in her early teens and was subjected to years of medical attention which she bore with fortitude, enjoying her life with her husband, Fred, and never complaining. Sadly she died at the age of forty-three in 1966.

Dorothy, however, had a great sense of fun and always welcomed us with a big-hearted smile. Grahame inherited her Celtic black hair and steady grey eyes. He greatly resembled her in looks and was also emotionally close to his mother. I remember my grandmother as an affectionate person who gave warm hugs. She always smelt fresh, probably having dabbed a little perfume behind her ears. I recall an occasion when I was called upon to wrestle with the ties of her corset, which kept her trussed and her waist quite firm. She often had a cigarette on the go, even when she worked in the kitchen. During the daytime she, typically for the times, wore a floral pinafore to protect her clothing, and a scarf fashioned as a turban. Something which fascinated me as a child were the florid bunions on her feet which she complained of, and which I have inherited, but otherwise she always seemed free of health problems. She had a naïve manner and was not given to engaging in, for instance, political discussion, but she was a wise and understanding mother to all her children.

In 1925 the family moved from 39 Belleville Road, London SW11 to a house in Surbiton for a job. Charles always managed to provide for his family and worked as a bus inspector. During the General Strike in 1926 he had to walk daily to the bus garage where he worked. He later became Chief Depot Inspector in charge of Kingston bus station where he was respected for his kindly efficiency by all the staff there. He died just before he was due to retire in 1955.

Withdrawn as he often seemed to his family, Charles was not without a sense of humour. Typical would be a situation where everyone was sitting at table having a meal and he would pick up a lemon, hold it in front of him and address it with a dead-pan expression saying "yer yellah". This rather 'Groucho Marks' style of humour was much appreciated in its day and Grahame and the younger children developed it as they grew older. At times they had a huge capacity for hilarity and Grahame and his siblings would see the funny side of a joke until the tears ran. This, among other things, bound them in a unity of understanding which held them together, and kept them loyal to each other, throughout their lives.

Charles, during the early years of Grahame's childhood, was involved in the high Anglican Church. He would attend the priest during church services as an Usher. This religious dedication transferred to Grahame who, in his early years, sang as a choir-boy and became an altar-boy when his voice broke. It was during this time that Grahame developed his all-consuming love of music. The sound of the church organ instilled a passion which never left him.

Grahame was often at odds with his father's obvious high principles and may have felt confused by some of his actions. They once found a watch in the street and Grahame fully expected to hand it in at the police station. However, Charles did not report the find and what happened to it Grahame never knew, but the watch was never seen again.

Grahame had a sense of humour which was rather self-deprecating and this made his stories very amusing. He recounted a story of how his father took him to the zoo as a birthday treat. The trip on the bus was free as Charles worked for the bus company. They probably went to Regents Park Zoo which still exists in London to this day. Upon arriving at the zoo the 'treat' involved standing outside and looking through the fence at the animals inside. Probably he couldn't afford the cost of going in through the turnstile. Whenever my father told this story I would end up laughing and crying all at the same time. The pathos was incorporated in a slow build-up, his anecdotes always being drawn-out. He could create a story from some very small incident and I was always held in rapt attention.

There seems to be conflicting memories about the facts of the following episode. Dorothy apparently formed a romantic attachment with the local butcher which Charles eventually became aware of. His discovery of her infidelity was catastrophic. Enid has recalled an episode of violence and an attempted suicide by Dorothy who was, as a result, admitted to a nursing home. The children, without their mother around, needed to be cared for and Enid remembers a very unpleasant woman called Alice coming to the house for a period. Enid and Grahame spent some time with Charles' sister, Florrie, who owned a bookshop in Wimbledon. They both benefited from her love of books and literature whilst living there. Audrey, aged 5, was looked after by a Mr Naish who was a colleague of Charles, and Marie, who was only 2 when these events unfolded, probably stayed with her mother in the nursing home. Grahame, aged 7, with his close emotional ties to Dorothy, remembered this as a dark period in his life. Enid recounts that, possibly because of the emotional stress; he became terrified of the Toby Jugs which stood on the dresser of a house he stayed at in West Barnes Lane around this time.

Eventually, after about a year, Dorothy was able to return home and resume her role as mother and wife. It would seem that her own relatives offered her little emotional support, but, in order to ease the burden of childcare and anxiety for Dorothy, the family moved in with Charles' parents at 16 Winsham Grove SW1. Enid recalls that Grandpa Young was very kind to her mother and "wouldn't let her do too much" and a Mrs Morgan came to help.

In July 1929 John was born and was just 9 months old when both Enid and Marie became ill with rheumatic fever. Both were taken to the Queen Victoria Hospital in Tite Street, Chelsea.

There can be few things in life that would totally demoralise a family more than the death of one of the children. Marie did not recover from her illess and she died on 3rd

September 1930 when Grahame was 9 years old. Charles was a husband who, while he no doubt felt the sorrow of his child's death deeply, did not seem able to give comfort to his wife. Grahame often came across a grief-stricken Dorothy kneeling beside a trunk which held things that reminded her of Marie. She would reach out to Grahame and I feel sure he gave her that needed comfort with deep sensitivity. Mother and son formed a bond, during that time, which was maintained for as long as Dorothy lived. The sadness of that time never left Grahame. In 1976 he wrote the following poem:

> Are there any left who remember
> My Mother's face as she looked
> At the flowers and said through
> Her tears "They remind me of Marie"?
>> I will always remember
>
> Are there any left who remember
> The sadness at the loss of
> A lovely child, a gentle child
> An angel child who, they said,
> Was too good for this world?
>> I will remember
>
> Are there any left who remember
> The beds of Marigolds which
> Flowered that year at Clapham
> As if in benediction - as if to say
> "Remember me. Remember me"?
>> I will always remember.

The family moved to 19 Green Lane in New Malden, Surrey in 1931 when Sibyl was born as Charles wanted the new baby to have a more permanent home. This was a terraced house, typical of the suburbs, with three bedrooms upstairs and a front lounge which was rarely used. The family usually congregated in the back room, adjacent to the kitchen, where there were armchairs in front of an open fire and a table for communal meals. A French window opened on to the back garden. A mangle for the washing was situated outside the kitchen door in a covered utility area. The back garden was long and narrow with a gate leading to an alley-way at the far end. This was home to Grahame for the remainder of his young life and, with exuberant brothers and sisters enjoying life together, was a very happy place to live until war broke out and everything changed.

My father held a wealth of deeply-felt principles and an impressive intellect. He could be quiet and brooding, and on the other hand talk in a protracted way about topics that some found controversial. No subject was barred and discussions with him could become quite heated. For this reason I would never have called him a popular man. He was difficult to know and never made any effort to win approval from anyone. His charm was a natural one and he opened himself to all provided they didn't expect him to make any compromise in his views. Those who appreciated his deep character really loved him and gained a lot from his honesty.

The thing that I was always aware of was how much he loved me. Tactile and reassuring, he gave me a strong sense of myself when I was little. As I grew older and my teenage angst baffled and infuriated him we often had strong arguments. A relationship which had fluctuated in many ways over the years ended abruptly when he was 66 and, diagnosed with lung cancer, died a few months later in October 1987.

The loss of him was, for me, like a deep wound that oozes slowly. At first I felt unaffected being busy with my own life and family. Gradually, with time, the sadness settled in me and I mourned him over many years. I found it hard to reconcile to myself all that had disappeared with him. It seemed impossible that so much wisdom contained within one person could cease to exist. Hardest to accept was that he was gone.

Grahame, Marie, Enid and Audrey 1925

Charles and Dorothy with Audrey,
Grahame, John and Sibyl 1933

Chapter 11

Grahame's young life, fraught with false starts and challenging emotional events notwithstanding, developed a deepening appreciation of things that he loved; music being one and his family another. His siblings definitely found him a supportive brother, but he did find it irresistible to tease people. Often he would ridicule something serious and, inappropriately, think this was hugely funny.

There are family stories, much repeated, which say more about the reason behind the story than the event itself.

Grahame's Anecdote 1:

Nelly Jelly's Party

"But she is having a party. She said she was. Why would she invite me if it wasn't true?" Six-year-old Audrey protested wildly and her mother spoke calmly. "But sweetheart, you didn't mention it before today. How and when did you hear about this party?"

"She came up to me in the playground at school and 'specially asked me" the little girl earnestly explained. "She said it was her birthday today and her mother said she could have a party. She is six, the same as me. Her name is Nelly and she's my

best friend." Audrey often created imaginary friends and was frequently teased by her big brother. Grahame, walked into the kitchen as the discussion was taking place. "So, will Nelly have some jelly at this party?" he sniggered.

Audrey sensed that, as the credibility of her story was now in doubt, there was only one course of action available to her. Bottom lip sticking out, eyes brimming with tears she turned slowly and walked out of the kitchen, head hanging. She hadn't even got halfway up the stairs before her brother called out. "OK, Ok. I will take you to Nelly Jelly's party."

Eyes gleaming with the victory won, and unshed crocodile tears, Audrey bounced around happily. "Thank you, thank you bruvvy wuvvy". Grahame understood that he had been manipulated, but he loved his younger sister and anyway he didn't want her to go to a strange house alone.

"What about a present?" her mother frowned doubtfully. She knew that the little girl in question came from a very poor family and wondered how they could afford to have a party. Their home was a few streets away and there was always a general unkempt air about the place.

Pushing aside her doubts, Dorothy set about making a pretty parcel for Audrey to take to the party; a new pair of gloves, bought with some precious saved housekeeping money, wrapped up in some floral drawer-lining paper and tied up with a hair bow. Shortly afterwards, true to his word, Grahame waited to accompany his little sister to Nelly Jelly's party. Audrey appeared at the front door glowing, all dressed up in her party frock, clutching the present and dancing from one foot to the other.

They made their way along the street, Grahame walking behind the little girl who was taking huge skips and jumps as she went along. When they got to the house there was no sign of a party in progress but, ignoring the discarded sink and general rubbish lying around the garden, they walked up the garden path and knocked on the front door. There was a long pause before the door was tugged open and an angry-looking woman peered out at them from a gloomy hallway. She held a cigarette between her lips and the smoke curled up into her hair which was tied up in rollers and wrapped in a scarf. She was wearing an apron and slippers. There was no party inside the house, no balloons, no music that would suggest party games, no other children.

"Yes?" snapped the woman who had probably been busy and seemed to resent their knocking. Silently, from a back room Nelly had appeared in the hallway and was peeping fearfully from behind her mother's legs.

"Er!" squeaked Grahame "nothing....my sister, she thought ..... Never mind". He lost his nerve and they turned around and walked back down the path and out of the gate.

Walking home in silence, Audrey holding Grahame's hand was subdued and thoughtful. Suddenly she stopped. "Wait a bit, I won't be long" she said and hurried back the way she had come towards the house. At the door, quietly and carefully, she placed on the step the present that she had brought for her friend Nelly. Then she slipped away unseen.

Whether Nelly Jelly actually existed, I am not sure. To my knowledge, no one who ever heard it doubted that this incident did occur. Audrey was also accused of stealing the cherries off some madeleine cakes set out for tea, but she always denied that.....

A poor scholar with erratic attendance due to ill-health, Grahame ended up in the remedial group at school. In fact his education appears to have been well below the radar and no opportunities for further studies, after leaving school, came his way for a long time.

The financial situation of the family and his lack of academic excellence, resulted in him leaving school aged 14. A large departmental store near London called Bentalls in Kingston in Surrey sometimes employed juvenile school-leavers. The young lad attended an interview for a job with his father. Charles would have seen a huge benefit to Grahame's starting to earn money and was pleased when he was accepted as a very junior employee. Grahame was bought his first pair of long trousers for the start of his new job.

Within the grand and historically acclaimed Bentalls Store was the Pets department in the basement:

Grahame's Anecdote 2:

The Pet Department

Grahame stood slightly hunched and nervous. The large hall of the Pet Department stretched before him. Sounds and smells which accompanied captive animals assailed him. They didn't have any pets at home, and he could find no real enthusiasm at the prospect of a close association with them.

"Well lad. Who might you be?" A somewhat rotund but well turned-out man in his mid-fifties approached him from behind.

"Grahame, Sir." His voice changed pitch embarrassingly as he spoke.

"Grahame, Mr Devonport Sir. How old might you be?"

"Fourteen and a half Mr Devonport Sir." Again the unplanned change of pitch made his response seem comical.

"Ee gods! They'll be sending them in nappies soon."

"Yes Sir Mr Devon......."

"Yes, Yes. Ok. Come with me. I'll show you where you are going to be working."

Grahame followed. The rather ample bottom waddled ahead of him and the boy realised with horror that he had fixed his lowered eyes upon it as they walked the entire length of the Departmental Hall.

Arriving at an area decorated to resemble an aquatic scene, his companion stopped.

"Here we are Grahame. This is the aquarium display."

Grahame looked up to where a painted Neptune fixed his angry gaze down from the walls accompanied by some winsome, but decently covered, mermaids. The floor was almost entirely taken up by an enormous pond within which *various statues stood. Standing to one side was a young man aged about twenty-five.*

"This is Clifford. You will be working together. Clifford, show Grahame the ropes will you?"

Grahame winced slightly as his new colleague sauntered up to him but was immediately put at ease by a big smile and warm brown eyes.

"Welcome to the fun factory. How are you at fishing?" Clifford put a reassuring hand on his shoulder.

Ten minutes later Grahame was clad in a similar way to his new friend; waterproof dungarees, size-nine wellington boots and holding aloft a long-handled fishing net.

"Now, when a customer comes into the department and a particular goldfish takes their fancy, we use our speed and agility to catch it in the net before it swims away. Got it?" Clifford obviously felt that no further training was necessary and Grahame waded into the pond alongside him.

As the morning wore on into the afternoon, a slow trickle of customers came and went. Clifford displayed his greater expertise by consistently targeting the desired fish and bringing it wriggling in his net to a point where the customer could receive it in a glass bowl

"Come on Gray! Move yourself." Clifford egged him on to ever greater efforts, doubling up with laughter when Grahame landed flat on his back, booted feet up in the air.

Grahame stood at the centre of the pool when a man came to the edge holding the hand of a small girl. Pretty in pink with a Shirley Temple hairstyle, she pointed into the water.

"I want that one Daddy." The child indicated a gold and black fish that swam close to where Graham was standing. With a bound Grahame was upon it, the net positioned to scoop up his prey. Momentarily losing sight of the creature, a sickening crunch underfoot left him in no doubt; the poor fish had not escaped his size-nine boot.

The momentum took Grahame across the pond, aided by the slippery mess of the crushed goldfish. Statues keeled over in a tidal wave created by his fall as he skidded to a halt. The aquatic pond had turned into a stormy sea and water heaved over the perimeter on to the feet of the waiting customers.

Water weed decorating his hair, Grahame smiled up at the man and his daughter. "Is there another fish that catches your eye?"

Clifford was helpless with laughter as Grahame hauled himself out of the water. Together they fought to keep straight faces as the ample frame of Mr Devonport approached, but both knew that working together would probably be a lot of fun.

In fact Grahame found himself working in many different departments over the following years of employment at Bentalls. The tense hierarchy system never really suited his nature and he failed to acquit himself well within the retail environment. However, he developed a great fondness for the store itself and also with the character and the history entwined within the majestic building.

Aged 17 and having been greatly affected by the church during his life thus far, Grahame attended an induction course at Kelham Theological College in Newark, Nottinghamshire. This was entirely of his own volition as he had become convinced that his true vocation was to be as a priest. He may have been seeking approval from his devout father, but this was not forthcoming as Charles did not approve of his plans to attend Kelham as a student.

Kelham Hall was owned by the Society of the Sacred Mission, an Anglican religious order founded in 1893 by Father Herbert Kelly. The Society purchased the building in 1903 and it became a theological college for Church of England priests. The Society had been involved in ministries throughout the world and in 1902 had started missions in South Africa engaging in pastoral and educational work. Kelham Hall became the centre of the organisation for the first sixty years of its existence.

After 1924 there was accommodation for 100 students which was extremely Spartan with no lighting, except oil lamps, and no heating or water above the ground floor. However, in 1939 a new living area for monks and students was opened which might have given Grahame the opportunity to spend some time there. The lovely gardens and playing fields were attractive features.

The Course Grahame attended was only for approximately a week or so and his good friend Ernest Chown had come to join him. It was a memorable occasion on two counts. Firstly he slipped over in the snow and knocked out his front tooth, and secondly he and Ernest became determined to study to become celibate priests. The family were extremely concerned when Grahame returned home minus a tooth and Charles seems to have been very suspicious of Grahame's association with Ernest, maybe suspecting that this was potentially a homosexual liaison. In any event, Grahame maintained his friendship with Ernest; a young man with a gentle disposition, who eventually did go on and become a priest. Whatever his resolve at the time, Grahame never pursued his religious vocation, and didn't return to Kelham Hall for any follow-up training. Ernest went on to study at St Stephen's House in Gloucestershire.

Chapter 12

The Second World War brought an unpredicted change in Grahame's life, as with many young men and women of his generation. The opportunity to fight for one's King and Country was enticing to the young and Grahame turned 18 on 17th July 1939 thus making him eligible to sign up without parental consent. However, Charles had a desperate fear of this very thing occurring. His own younger brother, George, had been killed in the trenches at Ypres in the First World War. He was a talented and trained singer, and the pride of his family. George's death had brought untold misery to his siblings who would never forget the misery of that war. Charles himself had signed up at Battersea on 5th February 1916 as a member of the Royal Flying Corps in WW1, and was painfully aware of the dangers to be faced during wartime. When an army recruitment officer knocked on the door of 19 Green Lane, he found himself face-to-face with a very hostile and aggressive father. It has been reported by family members that Charles took a swing at the man and sent him firmly on his way. No doubt he hurried back down the garden path and out through the gate with no thought of engaging in any further discussion on the matter.

In the end however Grahame did sign up to the British forces. He was most likely persuaded by the knowledge that engaging in the recruitment process voluntarily gave him certain options which might not exist if he waited to be conscripted later. He chose the Royal Air Force like his father and was enlisted on a training programme at RAF St Athan in the Vale of Glamorgan in South Wales.

The station had officially opened on 1st September 1938, and in 1939 its activities were extended with arrival of the new fighter group pool as a School of Air Navigation and Maintenance unit. During the war over 14000 personnel, both air and ground crew were trained at St Athan. A dummy airfield was built, using wood and cardboard, a few miles west of the airfield in an effort to disguise the actual site. This was largely successful as the Germans attacked the decoy airfield on a number of occasions and it had to be rebuilt each time.

Grahame, as a lowly Aircraftman (AC) in the RAF, had no aspirations to become a pilot. His opportunity was to be able to learn about all the new types of fighter planes that were being manufactured at that time. During his training as a mechanic he became familiar with the Lancaster Bomber, Hurricane and Wellington and, most exciting of all, the Spitfire.

The 20-month training program, which still exists today for young men enlisting with various RAF administrative units, was probably created in war-time circumstances. Grahame seems to have been present in the United Kingdom for a couple of years and during that time enjoyed periods of home leave.

Enid had made the decision to join the Navy and was stationed in London as a Wren within the Administration unit. The two were on home-leave at the same time when they decided to go for a bike ride together to Hampton Court. This took them some distance away from Malden. As they made their way home, they saw aircraft flying overhead and smoke rising in the distance causing them to take shelter under a hedge. When all was clear, quickly picking up their bikes, they made for home. As they topped the brow of a hill overlooking the residential area, they saw that German bombs had been dropped in the vicinity of Green Lane. They learnt later that about ten houses had been raised to the ground, one of them belonging to the family of Grahame's friend Norman who lived close to Number 19 which seemed, at first sight, undamaged. However, the rear part of the house had been badly blasted and no outside walls were left. Enid has reported that the family had a lucky escape. When the bombing started, Charles had stayed upstairs resting his bad leg, but Dorothy and Audrey ran downstairs with John and Sibyl. They all took shelter behind the sofa which protected them and which, when the bombing was over, was discovered to be pocked with shrapnel. The house being uninhabitable, the family went to stay with Grandpa Young until repairs had been completed and they could move back. Grahame and Enid returned to their units.

Sibyl remembers this as a frightening time in her life, not lessened by her big brother John who often teased her in the dark cupboard-under- the-stairs. The two of them, placed there at night for their safety, chatted and giggled until suddenly John would become mysteriously quiet. "John…. John…. Speak to me John." Sibyl plaintively begged. "Are you dead John?" The little girl became more and more agitated by his stillness until the naughty boy leapt up yelling to scare her even more. Eventually, like other children of similar age, John and Sibyl were evacuated to safer places and they went to stay with Auntie Florrie and Uncle Frank in West Bay, Dorset.

During this period Grahame was often able to spend some time with his younger siblings and John recalled rough handling at the hands of his brother. Grahame, aged 19, brought home some boxing gloves, one day, and announced his intention to teach the 10 year-old John how to box. This turned out to be a painful learning process for John who was about half the size of his brother. The lesson apparently involved Grahame holding one arm out, nonchalantly preventing John from landing a hit. If by some chance he did manage a lucky punch retribution from Grahame was severe. Many poundings in the back garden may not have taught John much about the sport of boxing, but it told him a lot about Grahame. In future years the brothers would share memories of this time and laugh at the uneven match and how Grahame took unfair advantage.

The circumstances which brought Grahame into the war are not set down and details as to how it was that he found himself boarding a troop ship headed for Burma in 1942 are unclear. The war in the Far East had started in December 1941 at the time of the Pearl Harbour bombing. The Japanese had captured Hong Kong and their army advanced into the Malay Peninsula, the Philippines and the Dutch East Indies. Malaya was overrun and Singapore fell in February 1942 when the Japanese continued their progress into Burma. This was a challenging involvement for British and Indian troops as they mounted their first offensive in the malarial ridden coastal region of Arakan. Defending troops became seriously undermined and demoralised whilst fighting during a retreat through thick jungle terrain over huge distances. The troops relied on the Royal Air Force for support as they penetrated deep behind the Japanese lines in central Burma.

On 6th December 1941 one of the largest convoys ever assembled, sailed from the Clyde bound for the Far East, carrying approximately 400 men of the RAOC and a large number of RAF servicemen. A number of escort vessels were assigned by the Royal Navy. They first docked in Cape Town after a two-week voyage.

Grahame had his first glimpse of a land the beauty of which he can have only imagined in his life thus far. Table Mountain and Table Bay at dawn must have given all the young airmen cause to stand in awe on the deck of that ship and later Grahame spoke of the 'table cloth' of cloud which drifted down over the astonishing mountain.

The convoy ships always put into Cape Town in order to stock up on essential commodities and fruits and vegetables. An abundance of foodstuffs were grown in Southern Africa but no longer available during wartime in Britain where strict food rationing was in place. The British troops were popular with the local people and dozens of cars were always waiting at the dock gates to take the young men on trips to the top of Table Mountain. At that time the Cable Railway Station was situated at the end of a very rough mountain road and the cable car made an alarming swinging ride to the top of the mountain. Later Grahame was to recall looking out over Table Bay from the mountain with a young attractive woman whom he met during his short stay in Cape Town.

Two weeks aboard the troop ship had brought the men close together and camaraderie had built up between Grahame and those with whom he shared the voyage. They gave each other nicknames and a special humour marked their time. However, conditions on board were cramped and some reported that the troop ships were contaminated with lice and vermin which undoubtedly made life very uncomfortable. I can't imagine Grahame quietly putting up with any biting insects.

One amusing anecdote told by Grahame was how one of the men named Harry had owned a trumpet with which he tormented his fellow passengers by playing it discordantly and loudly on frequent occasions. The trumpet had been the subject of many complaints throughout the voyage, but Harry was not a reasonable sort of guy and played the trumpet regardless of the reaction. The time came when it was Harry's turn to go on shore leave in Cape Town and while he was absent some fruit sellers approached the ship on bumboats to sell their wares. This was the chance the men had been waiting for and they purchased a large bunch of bananas and hefted it on to the deck. By way of barter the boys on the bumboat were offered Harry's trumpet as payment. As Grahame recounted, the exchange was a satisfactory one as the off-key sounds of the trumpet being played by its new owners could be heard during their departure back across the harbour. When Harry returned to the ship his friends called out to him as he arrived. "Hey Harry! Do you like bananas Mate?" Harry said that he did indeed like bananas. "Well that's good because you own a whole bunch of them!" It was never made clear whether Harry managed to eat all his bananas by himself as a typical stem will consist of many tiers each holding about 20 fruit and weighing between 30-50 kilograms.

John and Sibyl 1941

Chapter 13

The convoy of troop ships sailed out of Cape Town destined for Durban further up the East Coast of South Africa. It is likely that they encountered extremely rough seas as they travelled through the Cape of Good Hope and there are many reports of hazardous seas experienced by ships on this passage, especially during the winter months. Enemy Japanese submarines often patrolled these waters when escort ships were at their most vulnerable.

As they entered the safe harbour the men were probably serenaded by the famous 'Lady in White' who sang for the benefit of troopships passing in and out of Durban docks. Perla Siendle Gibson was a South African soprano who became internationally famous during the WW2. Born in Durban in 1888 she was the daughter of a local shipping agent who was of German descent. The busy waystation in Durban saw many convoys bound for North Africa and the Far East and men later reported her as a figure, clad in white, standing on a spot at the mouth of Durban Bay where ships entering and leaving the port would pass quite close. She sang patriotic songs through a megaphone which British soldiers had presented to her.

Upon docking in the safe Durban harbour Grahame's story takes a strange twist of Fate.

Grahame's Anecdote 3:

A Trip Ashore in Durban

Grahame and a friend went on shore-leave. They were collected from the ship by some local farmers. These pro-British South Africans would often pick up British servicemen and take them back to their houses for a meal and some entertainment. When they left the farm at the end of the visit they were given a bunch of bananas, as a gift, to take back to the ship. As they returned to the ship by foot through the streets towards the docks Grahame and his friend were confronted by Afrikaner youths. Always willing to fight an imagined foe, and seemingly trading brains for biceps, these young men were primed for aggression. The German blood in their veins and a cultural memory of the suffering of their kin at the hands of the British in the Boer War gave them a special hatred of the 'boys in blue'.

"Yirrah man! You gonna suffer now" said one of the thugs with a menacing air.

The two British airmen stopped abruptly and braced up to the threat, but the 'Brylcream boys' were puny in comparison to their assailants and, conveying a silent message to each other, turned on their heels and took off; desperate to escape. Both ran zigzagging, pursued with vigour by the more substantial youths and Grahame, always prone to mishap, skidded and tripped in the dusty street. As he fell he sensed a crack and felt a fierce pain shoot up his thigh. His leg was broken quite badly.

Seeing Grahame lying on the ground, leg askew and in obvious pain, the two Afrikaners quickly understood that the situation had become serious in a way that they might suffer consequences. They turned and left taking the precious bananas with them.

Sometime later, in a 'Whites only' Durban hospital, Grahame was visited by his regretful friend who sat by his bed and told him:

"The unit is leaving tomorrow, mate. You won't be with us."

Grahame was in despair when he thought of all the fun and action his friends might enjoy. The young men had anticipated thrilling experiences when signing up to join the Royal Air Force. This was not one.

"I haven't even got me knees brown yet" he lamented, looking down at his rather skinny white leg which lay, alone, on the pristine hospital sheet. The other had been hoisted, encased in plaster, into a sling above the bed. He would be reclining thus for six weeks.

The resentment of the Afrikaans towards the British had its roots in the history of the second Anglo-Boer War which followed tensions created by the Jameson Raid; an attempt in 1895 by a member of the British Military to seize Johannesburg by force. The discovery of gold and the resulting expansion of the railways had served to threaten the rural way of life of the Dutch people. The flow of immigration, from Europe, of gold prospectors created urbanisation. Black labourers from the tribal reserves flooded to work in the mines of "Goli" (City of Gold) in Witwatersrand. British troops had been brought in to South Africa to defend Natal and The Cape and tensions rose which resulted in Paul Kruger demanding that the British withdraw from the Transvaal border. After a 48-hour deadline war was declared on 10th October 1899 and the Boers presented themselves as aggressors from the Cape right through to the Transvaal and the war served as a trigger to rupture the already tenuous relationship between the Afrikaners and the British. During this period Paul Kruger sought help from the German government. In 1900 the first stage of the war came to an end with the annexation of the Transvaal, but guerrilla war followed when Afrikaner rebels formed small mobile commando units to harass British troops. Prolonged efforts against the Boer fighters included deportation of prisoners to Ceylon and the burning of farmhouses to prevent supplies reaching the guerrillas who were hiding in their own familiar terrain. The sparse veld with isolated *kopjes* suited the Boers and they became a formidable foe to the British soldiers. Concentration camps were set up to hold wives and children of the guerrillas and many of them died through disease and malnutrition. By the end of the hostilities approximately 200 000 people were being held in these camps where overcrowded conditions increased their hardship. Liberal leader Lloyd George explained the concentration camps in a government debate:

> "It means that unless the fathers come in their children will be half-starved. It means that the remnants of the Boer Army, who are sacrificing everything for their idea of independence, are to be tortured by the spectacle of their starving children into betraying their cause".

Many of the Boer fighters changed their allegiance to avoid deportation but the harsh policy earned the enduring hatred of the British by the Afrikaner Nation. More than fifty were executed in the Cape Province which was British territory. Eventually Hertzog and Smuts drafted a ceasefire document, with terms of surrender. This was named the Treaty of Vereeniging which was signed on 31st May 1902. The British and the Afrikaners were now under one sovereign but with a huge loss of life and independence of the Boers.

As the 2nd World War progressed, none of the British troops stationed within South Africa saw any fighting action and for them the war would pass without serious encounter with the German enemy. The local men who had attacked Grahame and his friend were probably politically driven and members of the *Ossewabrandwag* (OB) group which supported Germany during the war. They worked actively to disrupt the war effort in South Africa and many unsuspecting servicemen were beaten up by their members.

The convoy sailed shortly afterwards and the ship that Grahame had travelled on was struck by a Japanese torpedo in the Bay of Bengal on its way to Burma. It is believed that none of the British troops on board were saved.

Upon his release from hospital, Grahame made his way by train through the interior of the Natal Region and deep into the Eastern Cape in order to re-join his Unit. He would have become aware of the rugged loveliness of the land in which he found himself. The diversity and immenseness of the terrain must have given him a deep sense of wonder as the obvious differences between Africa and what he knew of England unfolded mile upon mile. As his journey progressed he would have seen small African villages perched upon the hillsides, their tribal customs there for all to see; the black boys tending the herds of skinny cattle in the fields and women walking along with huge bundles balanced upon their heads. Along the way he would have heard the chanting songs of the dark-skinned men working on the railroad. The unrestrained and helpless laughter of a group of African men sharing a story would surely have captured his imagination. The strong and unmistakable smell of unwashed and hardworking bodies would have assailed his nostrils. These were the sights and sounds to which Kathleen had been born and brought up with. This was her Land.

His long journey eventually took him to join his Unit in Grahamstown. Perhaps the ironic coincidence of the name of the town gave him an increased sense of destiny.

The British RAF had established many Air Schools in South Africa, mostly situated in the Transvaal and Orange Freestate. The Grahamstown No 44 Air School was linked, and in close proximity to other Air Schools in the Eastern Cape and they were all connected to the G.H.Q office in Pretoria. An amusing description of the Grahamstown Air School as Grahame would have experienced it in 1942 is contained in a book written by Gordon Frost - *The RAF and me: Wartime Memories of a Stirling Navigator 1941-1946* published in 2000.

> "The grass field at Grahamstown belonged
> to a pre-war flying club to which the
> RAF, in co-operation with the South

African Air Force (SAAF), had added hangers, classrooms, messing and sleeping accommodation (Nissen huts). It had also acted pre-war as a staging post for RAF activities in the Empire. This was borne out by an old Vickers Virginia twin-engine bi-plane, complete with open cockpit, which had not taken to the skies in many a long year but spent its retirement battened down to the ground by ropes. It was an object of fascination for us would-be aviators. We climbed all over it and many a souvenir would have been liberated had there been any left. The school was run by the South Africans but with a senior RAF officer in charge of the course and, with a couple of exceptions, by RAF ground instructors. These were mostly ex-schoolmasters or members of the RAF's educational wing. In addition to the by now familiar subjects of dead reckoning theory and plotting maps and charts and aircraft recognition, new areas opened up, such as meteorology, compasses, radio navigation, photography and reconnaissance."

This small insight gives weight to the understanding that the atmosphere within the grounds of the Air School was quite relaxed with its role being to prepare pilots and navigators for a greater purpose within the War effort. Grahame's rank in the RAF was Airman, the first rung, but he had received training as an aircraft mechanic and as such worked as ground crew. These men are fleetingly mentioned by Gordon Frost:

> "All the aircraft were very old Ansons, some of which had seen war service in the desert. They were dilapidated and shabby, the airstream whistled through gaps in the fuselage and the rivets performed a merry dance in the wings. They were started up by hand with starting handles, cranked by long-suffering ground crew and once in the air the undercarriage had to be wound up by hand and then down again when it was time to land."

Later, when recounting the rigours of his labours within the flight area, Grahame would tell of an unhappy event when he was standing in the hanger doorway, undoubtedly day-dreaming and thus unaware, when an aircraft edged its way past him. He found himself alarmingly lifted from his feet as the aeroplane wing clamped him by the head to the hanger door as it trundled outside. The air crew unaware of the incident carried on heedlessly. Grahame was profoundly shocked by his injury which required two stitches behind his left ear. Later he would identify this as his "war wound" and proudly display the scar to anyone who showed any interest.

Chapter 14

Daily life in the camp was probably maintained at a fairly leisurely pace for the men but wartime action was always expected. A diverse mix of personnel was recorded in the War Diary held in Pretoria as at 30th September 1942 which shows that 122 officers and 808 other ranks were resident at Air School 44 on that date. Permanently based personnel recorded were 70 SAAF, 206 Trainees, 27 bomb range personnel, 20 motor transport personnel, 8 medical orderlies, 10 in the fire section, 28 signal section, 14 police scrutinisers and runners, 18 Armourers and 28 Caterers and sundry personnel. The rest, perceived to be available for defence training, were 379 other ranks made up of 83 NCOs and 296 Airmen. Specific concerns were recorded on 14th October 1942, and are now held in the National Archives:

> "Organised sabotage has been carried on in various parts of the country by subversive elements whose activities may extend to this Station at any moment.
>
> Enemy aircraft based on hostile vessels have reconnoitred the coast and aerial attack, followed by attempted occupation of the Station by parachute troops, must be anticipated.

Enemy attack on the Coast is expected in which case infiltration of Commandos of enemy shock troops will occur."

Security procedure was set down as follows:

Intention:
No 44 Air School will defend the Air Station and Landing Ground against any form of attack or sabotage and maintain the operational serviceability of the Station.

Method:
- Security Fence: encloses the Petrol Storage, Hangers, Technical and Admin Buildings
- Patrols NMC: out of working hours a guard of NMC will patrol the perimeter of the security area
- Guards: First resident brigade will mount a 24 hour guard of 1 NCO and 3 ORs each on the main camp gate and the main security gate
- Inlying Picquet and Machine Gun Crews: strength 1 officer, 1 flight officer and 48 ORs
- Fire Picquet: strength 6 from Station personnel weekly and 5 permanent crew
- AFV Tp: strength 30

Grahame would have come under the description of OR (Other Ranks) and his involvement in any defence action undefined.

Grahame's memories of his life within the Station would lessen in time due to his fairly sedentary involvement. No doubt his working day had its ups and downs and he did recall the rather tenuous duty of starting up aeroplanes by pulling sharply down upon the propeller. This may require several attempts and there was always the risk of a kick-back and possible injury. Grahame had been given a gold ring as a gift by his father, before leaving the United Kingdom, which he wore permanently and valued greatly. However, he removed it and stopped wearing it altogether after an incident in which an airman lost a finger whilst starting up the engine of an aircraft in this way.

One can only surmise that, within a few months of arriving at the Station in Grahamstown, Grahame's leisure interests diverted to those he could find outside the Camp when he was able to take leave and visit the town.

Although they lived in the same town the chance of Grahame and Kathleen meeting each other would come about only if some kind of time-frame in which their worlds would converge should happen. This was unlikely considering the age difference; Grahame having turned 21 in July and Kathleen still only 15 years old. But it did happen when they first saw each other in a church, near to where Kathleen lived, which both had attended one Sunday each accompanied by a friend. After the service they spoke and Grahame asked if Kathleen would like to accompany him for a milk-shake at the nearby Ramona Café. Kathleen agreed, knowing that her mother would not approve, but hoping to get away with it. Unfortunately her brother John, who sang with the church choir, spotted her and ran home to report her to their mother. The story goes like this:

Grahame's Anecdote 4:

Grahame meets Kathleen

Grahame could tell that Kathleen was much younger than him but was fascinated by an untamed and engaging quality about this, apparently, reckless girl. Sitting at a table in the café he watched her animated face as she chatted to him, swinging her legs on the high legged chair. She was very pretty and wore a cotton frock which made her seem even younger than her 15 years.

Suddenly her expression froze mid-sentence. She had been enjoying the enthralled attention of this uniformed young man and had been giving him the full benefit of a long and complicated story.

"Oh, Gott. There's my Mother!" she exclaimed and jumped off her stool.

Standing in the doorway was a handsome, but rather forbidding-looking woman. She wore a floral pinafore and her arms were akimbo; fists clenched at her waist. Wordlessly she stared across the room at Kathleen. Then, having conveyed her message, she turned around and left abruptly. Grahame stood watching as the mother, quickly followed at a trot by her daughter, walked away down the road. Kathleen hadn't even said goodbye - not even a wave.

Grahame paused, paid for the milkshakes, and then he also took off down the street after the striding woman. He tried to engage her in conversation on the way but all efforts were met with a stony silence. Shortly they arrived at a Dutch-style homestead with a covered porch at the entrance. Mother and daughter clumped up the wooden steps, entered the house, and Grahame, without seeking any invitation followed them through the door. Inside was a neat home and the delicious smell of cooking, which drifted from the kitchen, gave the young airman a nostalgic reminder of his own family left behind in far-off England.

Hester stood back as they entered the kitchen where the rest of the family regarded the sudden appearance of Grahame with some surprise. Kathleen said, in Afrikaans, to her father "Mother has let an RAF chap in", then disappeared up the stairs to her bedroom and didn't emerge again for fear of reprisal. The children, present in the house, viewed this uniformed stranger with unconcealed amazement; mouths hanging open. Robert, however, responded with great pleasure and his face lit up; delighted to see an Englishman. With true South African hospitality he ushered Grahame to take a seat and the two men sat together talking at the kitchen table.

Later on in the evening Hester entered Kathleen's room and said, "You had better go and say goodnight to your friend". There was no anger, no recriminations because Hester had warmed to this insistent young man.

Grahame missed the bus back to Camp that night and would do on many more occasions in the future.

And so it was that Grahame became a regular visitor to the house in Beaufort Street. Whenever he had leave from camp, usually dressed in Khaki shorts and shirt, he would appear at the family home and be sure of a welcome. His subtle sense of humour was appreciated and his very English naivety often mocked, especially by Kathleen. He formed a strong relationship with Robert who, after a couple of drinks, would hold forth at length about political matters and the two men often sat at the kitchen table sharing their views. Grahame has recalled that on one occasion, while the old man was giving a particularly prolonged discourse, he started fiddling with a matchstick. He had, during dull periods at the Camp, been practising the art of flicking matches with some accuracy and was now able to shoot them some distance to hit a target. This now became a focus of his attention whilst listening to Robert facing him at the kitchen table and, almost without thinking he flicked a match using thumb and fore-finger. It flew across the table and lodged itself in Robert's ear. The sudden pain shocked Robert and stalled him long enough to allow Grahame to dash off before being chased around the house and out into the yard.

Grahame often played with Cynthia who, in August 1942, turned four years old. He enjoyed teasing her and on one occasion gave her six raw eggs to eat because she said she wanted as many as her father had for his breakfast. Disgusted at the prospect she apparently made her feelings known to him by the threat: "I'm gonna spit at you just now!" Whether this deflected his teasing isn't known, but I am guessing not much.

Kathleen was allowed to maintain her friendship with Grahame with the full approval of Hester who developed a great affection for him. She was never comfortable with spoken English but seemed to form an understanding of the person he was. Love of music was always a dominating part of his character and he would listen, entranced, to classical concerts on the radio. Hester regarded this as rather quirky and observed with some amusement "Oh, he's forever listening to those sympathy concerts". She had never before been aware of the existence of the Symphony Concerts that he loved so much.

Meanwhile, Kathleen had an escort in Grahame to take her out to such entertainments as the *bioscope* (cinema) and, more enticingly, the local Dance at the Town Hall where the RAF men formed a queue to dance with each girl on a Saturday night. Grahame probably never managed to actually dance with the young Kathleen as she was whisked away from him as soon as they walked through the door. I can imagine that he stood waiting throughout the evening for the moment when the band stopped playing and it was, at last, time for him to walk her home. Her gaiety was infectious and she has recalled one occasion when one persistent young man, at her invitation, accompanied them along the road and took her attention as they chatted. Grahame apparently went into such a deep sulk that she learned a harsh lesson and never risked making him jealous again in the future.

Kathleen has recalled that the two of them did their 'courting' near the Monument in Grahamstown. There was a cafe surrounded by canons which they visited regularly and this was where they got to know each other well. Something in each of them complemented and completed the other.

Kathleen, though young had a very mature and rather 'earthy' way about her. She had come to regard life in a very practical way and was able to find solutions to apparently insurmountable problems. Nothing frightened her and she faced the world full-on, ready to fight the battles of those she loved. As her love for Grahame grew, he would have become aware of her completely unwavering confidence in the feelings she held for him. He must have become convinced that she would never let him down once he had gained her affection.

Grahame, in his life thus far, had experienced a lot that made him fearful and he was often anxious about small things. Never in his life had he met someone who carried life with such light-hearted ease the way that Kathleen did and he was completely fascinated by her. This genuinely honest young man would have been a novelty for Kathleen who had been primed to accept that she would, probably one day, marry an Afrikaans farmer with inherited land but not much intelligence. Grahame with his love of classical music and literature was something of an enigma to Kathleen, but she would never question those aspects about him, and she would always guard and protect his freedom to enjoy the things he loved.

And so their relationship strengthened to a point where, unlikely though it seems, they made a decision to marry. On Grahame's birthday; 17th July 1943, when he turned 22 and Kathleen was still only 16 years old, they were married in Grahamstown Cathedral with the full blessing of both Robert and Hester.

Chapter 15

A nd so there followed a time that Grahame would later describe as the 'Halcyon Days'. An idyllic period when he would visit Kathleen, walking from the Camp to town amongst the sweeping hillsides, and spending time with the girl he loved. He had to brave taunts from his colleagues who called him a "cradle snatcher", but he cared little about that.

The War Diary maintained at the Station between January and April 1943 registers a variety of noteworthy incidents, for example on 7th January an Oxford 3477 dived into the sea near Kowie and Lt. Lahner and 3 pupils were lost and the bodies not recovered. Pupils regularly left the station to attend courses at other Air Schools and some arrived in Grahamstown to attend courses as part of an on-going training programme. Air accidents seem to have happened with some frequency and the Anson aircrafts were involved in sea reconnaissance on a daily basis. Grahame has recalled an occasion where the men in his Unit were required to travel by Landrover to the scene of a crash and transport bodies back to the Base. He said that they carried the casualties across rough terrain from the wreck and, as he was holding a stretcher at the rear end, and following the man at the front, a snake slithered underneath the stretcher between him and the front carrier. Fortunately, the snake had gone by the time he reached the point at which he might have trodden on it. Yet again, a lucky escape!

There were certain entertainments for the benefit of the men and women resident at the Camp. On the 1st January the NEC and Engineers arranged a Sports Day, for the attested natives, which was to be patronised by the CO and other officers. On the 5th January, members of the Air School treated members of the First Division to tea and refreshments at the YWCA. On the 9th January the PDF Concert Party gave a creditable performance of "The Accelerators" in the YMCA hut. Various sporting activities were available such as rugby matches between Air Schools. An Airmen's tennis court was opened and on 4th April a match, Officers versus Airmen was held. (Officers won 98 to 78.) Grahame was fairly accomplished at cricket and was a member of a team which played wearing whites and full cricketing regalia. This must have looked a little incongruous in the middle of the African bush, and I don't suppose that much cricket was being played back in poor beleaguered Blighty!

In the meantime Kathleen was preparing for her wedding. She was very proud of the fact that she paid for her own wedding. I am sure that this was possible as she had a job at a well-patronised restaurant, but as this was wartime a lot of the normal wedding paraphernalia was not available to be bought. The wedding dress was made from a silk parachute and hand embroidered by a friend. This must have been a labour of love and the result was as unique as any *haute couture* design. Hester, in true Dutch style would have collected little items for her trousseau.

During Grahame's leave times the couple would walk around the old colonial areas of town and on one occasion arrived in front of a home from which the sound of Mozart could be heard being played on a piano. Grahame insisted on sitting on the wall outside to listen and was noticed by a lady who came outside to speak to him. When she understood how much Grahame was enjoying the recital this lady invited them both inside and when they left she said they were welcome to come back any time. I believe that Grahame became a regular visitor at that house where he was introduced to different composers and developed his keen ear for music.

Kathleen was always amused at Grahame's fascination with the African natives. He wanted to communicate with them and was always asking Kathleen how to say things in *Xhosa*. On one occasion he wanted to give an old woman a cigarette and Kathleen seriously instructed him to say, "stick this up your backside you old crone", in the native language. The furious response from the woman together with Kathleen's helpless mirth told Grahame that he had been tricked once again.

The Pass-Laws had been stringently upheld in the Eastern Cape since the Native Law Amendment Act of 1937. This meant that black Africans were required to live in Reserves and had to obtain a pass to allow them to enter the town by day in order to work. It was rare to see any black natives within the precincts of the town except during working hours. At night it was expected that all native Africans would return to their homes in the Reserve area. This situation was never questioned by Kathleen but her confidence in the prevailing system was seriously shaken when walking with Grahame one night. They were not far from the Camp when they noticed a black figure hiding in the bushes beside the path. The man was smiling broadly and completely naked crouching there in the dark. There was no obvious aggression, but Kathleen was as frightened by the incident as she might have been had he carried an *assegai*. There was never any explanation for the man's appearance although it was reported to the police. The activity of military aircraft and ballistic training in the area of the sacred *Xhosa* tribal lands might simply have driven this poor man mad.

And so the day of the wedding arrived. The couple were married in Grahamstown Cathedral which seems an exalted venue under the circumstances but it must be remembered that, although Grahame had no family living in South Africa, Kathleen had a huge number of relatives on both her mother and her father's side. On the day of the wedding the cathedral was full and the congregation included uniformed RAF personnel who arrived from the Camp. An Afrikaans style 'bush telegraph' had been set in motion and, in a country where no telephones existed and travel was limited due to the war involvement, it seems that people somehow knew of the occasion. Kathleen was thrilled to see her *Oupa* Coetzer (Martinus) again ten years after she had last seen him. He had apparently remarried and arrived with a young wife who was pregnant. They brought with them two children, a girl and a boy, and Hester privately thought that they were probably her half-brother and sister. Kathleen later observed that they were obviously poor as the young woman was wearing a cotton 'day dress'. Martinus was unhappy that he couldn't communicate with Grahame who didn't understand Afrikaans.

Grahame was wearing his blue RAF dress-uniform during the wedding, an image that brought to mind the prediction of the fortune teller visited by Kathleen when she was 12 years old in Knysna. She was attended by one solitary bridesmaid called Barbara, ever after known only as "my bridesmaid", and with who she remained in contact for the rest of her life.

Telegrams from England indicate that Grahame's family and friends sent their heart-felt congratulations. Though they seem to have initially believed that he was marrying a "black woman", photographs sent back home had reassured them that Kathleen was a pretty and mature young woman who could easily have been taken for 'the girl next door'.

The couple had their honeymoon in Port Alfred on the East Coast. This was always, and remains today, a popular holiday resort with a lovely beach and peaceful surrounding area. During war time there was aggressive enemy action against British shipping and the War Diary of 44 Air School has recorded that six Anson aircraft were engaged in searches, during that period, in the Port Alfred area looking for life-boats near to where wreckage and patches of oil had been sighted. This being the case, it is hard to know what kind of honeymoon accommodation was available for Grahame and Kathleen, but one supposes a small hotel. Both were virgins on their wedding night and Kathleen has recalled that Grahame approached his bride with glittering eyes and the words "Now you are all mine…" It is a shame that no-one took him aside before that night and suggested that he approach the situation a little more sensitively. As it was, the 16 year old Kathleen was so alarmed that she felt inclined to leave the nuptial bed and 'take to the hills'.

Hester recalled that after the honeymoon Grahame complained to her that Kathleen had been really cruel to him. Sitting on Port Alfred beach, Grahame, having failed to gain any colour from the hot South African sun, took his white body down to the water's edge for a swim. When he emerged dripping wet to take his place on a towel beside Kathleen, she said "I heard those people sitting over there talking. They were saying that they could see a pair of old braces floating in the sea. I think they were looking at you!" This story made Hester cackle with laughter.

As a married man Grahame was able to live in the town and travel daily to the Camp for his duties. The young couple were unable to stay at the family home at 45 Beaufort Street because Frank had recently become engaged, and hastily married, to Dolly who was pregnant. Thus there was no room for Grahame and Kathleen and they took lodgings nearby at 2 Napier Street with an English couple called Mr and Mrs Daniels. This was a very happy arrangement as the older couple became very fond of the newly-weds, and Peter, their son who was a little boy at the time, kept in touch with them for many years afterward.

The following year was unremarkable, except for the fact that Kathleen apparently suffered a series of health issues. She became pregnant at some stage but the pregnancy ended with a miscarriage one night and the Doctor was called out to their home. He attended to the basic removal of the foetus and informed Grahame that it had been a boy after flushing it down the toilet. Both were very upset and Kathleen ended up in hospital when it transpired that she had an infection. She has recalled that the nurses treated her coldly, believing that she had deliberately aborted the pregnancy which was so often the case when young women arrived in that ward. This event was followed by an ectopic pregnancy when she lost one ovary after an appropriate operation. She must have believed that her chances of becoming a mother were becoming quite slim. Later on the frequent occurrence of tonsillitis necessitated the removal of one tonsil; a common enough operation, but requiring a period of convalescence. During this time Kathleen's health must have been of concern to Grahame and photographs show that she became quite plump having put on some weight. During this period *Oupa* Coutzer sadly died, aged 77, and Kathleen travelled with Hester to attend his funeral.

The end of WW2 meant that the British forces left South Africa and were shipped back to Britain. Grahame left in September 1945 and Kathleen again took up her role of helping Hester with the children. She was to follow her husband at a later date on especially provided transport for wives of servicemen returning to the UK. Obviously it was quite usual for men at the Station to marry local girls, but not all had made a good judgement as some of the men already had wives and children waiting for them back home.

Aircraft Crash Collection Grahamstown Air School 44

Grahame with Robert, Hester, Dawn and Cynthia 1944

Grahame and Kathleen Grahamstown 1945

Chapter 16

If the truth were known, when it came to the time to leave South Africa, Kathleen felt quite ambivalent about the prospect of joining her husband who now seemed very far away. She had settled back into her life with family and friends and, being so young, didn't feel a strong sense of responsibility towards her role as a wife. She had not given birth to any children, and maybe had given up hope of ever becoming a mother.

On 30th December 1945 she writes her first entry of a diary:

> "Too much Andrews. Say goodbye all round. Hester walked home with me. I walked back with her, she walked back with me."

The "Andrews", which was the trade name for a make of liver salts, suggests that her stomach had become upset after a lively party with too much good food over Christmas. Kathleen appears to have developed a friendship with someone called Hester and she is not referring to her mother, in this case, as she was living at home at the time.

On the 1st January 1946 Kathleen travelled by train to Cape Town. She has recorded that on the way she passed through George and 'The Pass'. This would have been a very nostalgic journey which threw up many memories of her childhood spent in this area. On arriving at 9.45 in the morning she went straight to the docks and boarded the 'Carnarvon Castle', which set sail that same day at 5 pm. Her diary recounts how the first day at sea was rough as they travelled North-westerly in the South Atlantic and that very few people attended a life-boat drill held on deck. Kathleen herself, thankfully, did not suffer from sea-sickness.

The boat journey seems to have been fairly enjoyable for Kathleen who made friends with other women and one in particular called Pixie who, on Day One of the voyage, sat up late with her on deck on a "beautiful night". Porpoises were spotted. Concerts and Dances were held on board and on 10th January Kathleen and Pixie watched a film called "Irish Eyes are Smiling".

Boat drills seem to have been called regularly, during the first week, due to engine trouble. The ship, as a result, had to travel "very slowly". On 11th January the Diary reports a man overboard. Apparently this was the Ship's carpenter, Mr Perry, who was never found, despite assistance from another vessel. On 12th January a collection was made for Mr Perry's dependants. Kathleen reports that she was "feeling homesick" on 16th January. Presumably boredom was setting in and the reality of leaving South Africa was becoming clear as the weather became colder. A lot of time spent knitting has been recorded in the diary. Kathleen would have been made very aware of the necessity for warm clothing once they arrived in England.

On the 17th January Kathleen's diary reports a dramatic day:

> "Orders to wear our life belts all the time -
> from tomorrow danger of floating mines.
> Lady and baby died during the night. Bury
> baby at sea."

One can only guess at the tensions that were building on board the Carnarvon Castle as they approached the United Kingdom.

On 19th January Kathleen reports "feeling excited" and "going to the Bursar's Office to collect her Landing Card". She says that they played tombola for the last time and it was "Pixie and Mary's turn to bath". Then on the 20th January the diary reports their arrival at Southampton:

> "Arose feeling very excited. The Isle of
> Wight in sight. Very foggy. Docked at
> about 4. Saw Gray in the distance. He
> came onto the boat for a few minutes.
> Wonderful to see him. Queued up until
> 12.15 am to pass through Immigration.
> Managed to get down gang-plank sooner
> than expected. Met Mum at Waterloo.
> Got home at about 1.30 pm. Very Cold.
> Met Audrey, John, Sibs and Dad. Feeling
> very tired and strange."

And so Kathleen had arrived in the United Kingdom and Grahame's family gave her a warm welcome. She was taken to 19 Green Lane in New Malden, Surrey, where evidence of the destruction by bombing must have been all too real.

Post-war England was, undoubtedly, a bleak place in the middle of winter and the country was still reeling from the effects of the War. Upon alighting from the train from Waterloo Kathleen observed that the moon seemed very bright. In fact what she was seeing was a weak sun which occasionally broke through the fog. She was completely unused to the fact of winter and believed that someone had been sprinkling salt on the ground. What was actually frost had previously been experienced by her only in the Highlands of the Eastern Cape in the early mornings during the short winter months.

The diary which had begun at the start of her adventure continues for a few months. This indicates a mixture of the excitement of a new life and intense homesickness. On 23rd January she writes:

> "2nd letter from Mummy. Grahame and I
> went to the food office. I get my Ration
> Book."

Food rationing must have been a complete anathema to Kathleen who loved to eat without restraint. It had been started in England in June 1942 by the Combined Food Board to coordinate the worldwide supply of food to the Allies. By August 1942 practically all food items were rationed apart from vegetables and bread, which were limited in supply, and imported fruit during the war years practically ceased. Some British children who had adjusted to the restrictions did not even know that bananas existed. A popular music hall song "Yes, We Have No Bananas" highlighted the irony of the situation. Some sellers imposed their own restrictions on food purchases and sometimes customers were not able to buy basic commodities. Most controversial was the sale of bread which was not rationed until after the war had ended. An Order was passed which said that bread could not be sold on the day it was baked because stale bread could be "sliced more thinly" thus reducing consumption. With an austere economic climate after the War and frequent strikes by dock workers things became worse and a ration-book fraud arose where, in some instances, the ration allocations of the dead were being claimed by the living.

Small wonder that the British people had become very tense about the fair distribution of food and Dorothy had been battling to feed her young family adequately for a very long time. The first sign of friction between Dorothy and Kathleen came when Kathleen liberally sprinkled precious sugar all over her morning porridge.

Kathleen's Diary continues in a very cryptic way. On some days she is full of enthusiasm about new experiences and excitement at meeting new family members. On 24th January she writes:

> "Grahame and I go up to London to meet Enid at Charing Cross Station. Terrible lunch. Meet Enid. Went to Lyons for coffee. Saw Palace, St James' Park, The Mall, Ritz, Regents Street, Piccadilly Circus. Nice Day."

Enid and Kathleen seem to have become immediate friends because there are many entries where they meet to go shopping and, although Enid was obviously still working in the WRNS and had been actively engaged in a "special job" in France, they appear to have chatted on the phone regularly.

Grahame was stationed with the RAF base at Aston Down in Chalford in Gloucestershire and Charles wrote to him saying:

> "I can truthfully say that Kathleen has already endeared herself to every one of us and I sincerely hope that the future will bring added happiness to you both."

He wished Grahame luck with his forthcoming exams and encouraged him to see that, whatever the outcome it will be "something attempted, something done which will bring results sooner or later". This was fairly prophetic as Grahame went on to study as part of a Government programme which led him on to qualifying as an F.R.I.C.S. (Fellow of the Royal Institute of Chartered Surveyors).

Meanwhile, Kathleen was still living at 19 Green Lane. She reports going for a bike-ride with John one day: "very muddy" and going to tea at Wimbledon with Auntie Doris. On 2nd February she met Enid at the bus stop and the family came for the evening: "We danced and played Pit. Very happy evening."

On 7th February Enid and Kathleen went to West Bay in Bridport, Dorset to visit Auntie Florrie and Uncle Frank. Grahame joined them the following day. It would seem that this was a very special holiday and Kathleen seems to have enjoyed it very much. West Bay had a particular significance to Grahame and Kathleen who later visited Auntie Florrie and Uncle Frank many times over the years. Uncle Frank, apparently a fairly accomplished poet, wrote the following which best describes this beautiful place in the South West of England:

> There's miles of bluest ocean
> Where the burning sunlight gleams
> But it's not the ocean only
> That leaks into my dreams
> There's a wee Stay, wild with breezes
> Where the sweeping gulls are calling
> And the sea can never sleep
> A wee Bay - a West Bay
> Tossed with swirling foam
> With scarce a half a mile inland
> The spot we've planned for Home

Grahame renewed his friendship with his old friend Ernest who had fulfilled his aim to become a priest and appears to have been very supportive towards Kathleen during the early months of her arrival in England. Kathleen's Diary reports that:

> "Ernest arrived. Went to Palais.
> Came home 10.30 pm."

On 22nd February the Diary records that "Sibyl and I went to Kingston had lunch. Mrs Chown phoned."

Mrs Chown is the mother of Ernest Chown who shows a genuine concern and interest in the wellbeing of Kathleen during the time that Grahame was stationed away. In fact this was a difficult time for Kathleen, despite the support from the family, and she frequently records how she is "missing Gray". The winter must have seemed long and the short dark days of the Northern hemisphere winter very strange. However, on the 25th March 1946 the Diary reports:

> "Gray phoned and told me that he has been demobbed."

The following - written like a normal day:

> Tuesday 26th March - "bunch of mail from home. Did some ironing. Had lunch at Civic. Went to Rec with John and Sibyl. John and I went for a ride on the bikes."

This was the very last entry in the Diary.

It is difficult to analyse how and why things deteriorated. Having Grahame at home must have, at first, seemed like a dream come true to Kathleen, but the young couple were suffering all the problems that might be expected when living with the family with no privacy for themselves. Grahame had always had a strong attachment to his mother; something alluded to by Hester before Kathleen left for the United Kingdom. With her deep intuition she seemed to understand the way he felt and said: "Always remember, my girl; if a man can't love his mother, he can't love anyone". Kathleen had not expected that she would begin to feel excluded, and her need to be her husband's 'only love' was very great.

Kathleen must have appeared like a spoilt child at times, trying desperately to establish her place in the world that she had come to, but the odds seemed stacked against her. It felt to her that Dorothy was judging her harshly, and Grahame was becoming torn between the demands of the two women he loved. She began to feel betrayed and her mind often returned to those wild African hills of the Eastern Cape. She became intensely homesick.

Things came to a head about six months after Kathleen's arrival. The Ministry of Defence had organised a ship that was made available to women who had realised their mistake in coming to England, for one reason or another, and now would like to return to South Africa. In the wake of a heated argument Kathleen made a decision to leave on that ship and go back to her family. However, before she took this step she phoned Ernest Chown from a public telephone box and told him all that she was suffering. How much she missed her mother and father, how Grahame was not supporting her, how angry she felt and how unfairly she had been treated. Ernest apparently spoke to her in such a way as made sense to her and changed her mind. She took out a rental of a small bedsit nearby and put down a deposit. Then she returned to Green Lane to pack her things.

Kathleen has recounted that she stood at the doorway holding her cases. She looked into the sitting room to where Grahame was sitting with Dorothy and said; "I am leaving, you can come with me if you want to." And he followed her.

Epilogue

Kathleen was like a colourful butterfly. Throughout her short diary there are entries referring to "having a manicure" so she always had beautiful nails and looked fashionable. Shortly after arriving in England she got a job in the Beauty Department at Bentalls in Kingston and worked there for a number of years. Grahame, with a view to furthering his career prospects, studied whilst working as a rent collector for an Estate Agent called Reed and Co. He took Articles and eventually qualified as a Chartered Surveyor.

Grahame and Kathleen were married for 44 years before his death in October 1987 at the age of 66. They had three daughters each born six years apart; Marilyn in September 1948, Pamela in September 1954 and Catherine in April 1961.

There were always huge differences in their views on life, having come from such different backgrounds, but Grahame and Kathleen drew together in their shared memories of Grahamstown and the Eastern Cape. Grahame had initially intended that they would return to South Africa to live but after the end of World War 2 the Afrikaner-dominated National Party (NP) and the *Broederbond*, which had steadily progressed with its ideology of racial segregation, forced legislation to legalise apartheid after a general election in 1948. This caused a situation where residential areas were created in order to divide racial groups. From 1960 to 1983, 3.5 million non-white South Africans were removed from their homes and forced into different neighbourhoods. Significant internal resistance and violence followed and unrest spread throughout the country. The Labour-ruled British Government, maintaining a strong stance against the regime, imposed sanctions and a long-term trade embargo against South Africa.

The political climate, volatile as it was, planted strong doubts in Grahame's mind about the future of South Africa. As he grew older the immorality of the system of Apartheid presented a dilemma, and over time Grahame became unwilling to seek employment and live in South Africa. Kathleen never stopped thinking about her family and the country of her birth, and she often suffered painful nostalgia, but the years went by and she settled down to the life of an English housewife. Bringing up the children became her main focus.

Then, in October 1970, when Catherine was 9 and old enough to be left for a short time, she travelled, by herself, back to South Africa. She had never flown in a plane before and, with a brand new British Passport, she travelled via Johannesburg to see her family in Port Elizabeth. This was such an event that three local newspapers sent reporters to interview her and take photographs.

"Time has not changed my parents much - in fact, I think I am the one who has aged". She is quoted as saying.

Her views on race were recorded as:

> "I have found that the man in the street in England would much rather have the cricket Springboks visiting Britain than all this political uproar."

Kathleen never judged the Apartheid system harshly and maintained a somewhat 'right wing' view throughout her life.

Kathleen's father, Robert, died in 1974 aged 74 then Hester died in April 1981 in Port Elizabeth Hospital. Kathleen had arrived in South Africa the week previous to her death and has said that she was able spend valuable time giving an emotional farewell to her mother. Kathleen reported that the *Xhosa* nurses who attended her sat at her bedside on the day that she died and sang traditional songs, knowing that she could understand their language. They stroked her hands and called her *Umama* (Mother).

Kathleen was only 61 when Grahame died aged 66 in 1987 after a short battle with lung cancer. It was devastating for her to lose her beloved husband and find herself alone, but she rallied her strong Afrikaans character and moved on with her life. She became active in fund-raising for the Cancer Research Society, and for a short while stood as Chairman. She travelled extensively, sometimes back to South Africa to visit her sisters. Her daughters gave her 8 grandchildren who all loved her and she became a strong part of their young lives.

There was never any suggestion that Kathleen would meet and marry anyone else after the death of Grahame. She remained true to him for 27 years until her own death aged 87 in April 2014.

She lived in a pretty place by the sea in Mudeford, Christchurch, in the South of England at the end of her life. With various health issues Kathleen found movement difficult, but neighbours reported that, the week before she died, she had been seen walking in the sunshine wearing a summer frock.

Robert (Happy) Petzer

Author's Note

I am the eldest of Grahame and Kathleen's children and felt compelled to write about the African part of their lives which to me feels like a fascinating story needing to be told. I was brought up in England with a strong awareness that half my extended family were from another country and that it was an exotic place, unlike anywhere in England. This I found to be true when I, myself, visited South Africa in my late teens, and much of my life has been spent in places in Africa. I came to recognise the different aspects of the very complicated racial structure in South Africa as well as further North, in Zambia and Zimbabwe where I lived for many years.

My Mother's position of being both English speaking and from Afrikaans heritage was rather unusual, and the intriguing history that leads to that circumstance, I discovered as the book developed.

Stories have been told to me since I was very young, and I have used my imagination to bring life to these anecdotes. I have written in italics where the actual scenarios are not known.

When I started writing this book Kathleen, my mother, was still alive and I sat with her on many occasions recording, with a tape recorder, her childhood recollections. As she grew older her memories seemed to go back further and she could remember the most remarkable details about her youth.

The record of Grahame's childhood written in Part 2 is a mixture of family anecdotes and the input from his sisters Enid and Sibyl. Memories of individuals do not always tally and, as there is a wide age-gap between these two siblings, recollections of events do sometimes differ. However, a combination of a deeply felt wish to keep faithful to the truth and the desire to remember loved-ones kindly has brought us to consensus.

Thanks to Sibyl Bartlett and her efforts in editing the shambles of my first literary attempt.

I give many thanks to my husband Jon who has been an avid and interested reader of each Chapter as it unfolded. He remains my 'number one' (my only) fan.

Sources of Information

Books

The Making of South Africa by M.S. Green (pub. 1967)

In Search of South Africa by H.V. Morton (pub. 1979)

Cape Colony Today by A.R.E. Burton (pub. 1907)

The White Tribe: South Africa in Perspective by David Harrison (pub. 1981)

Conversation s with Myself by Nelson Mandela (pub. 2011)

Long Walk to Freedom by Nelson Mandela (pub. 1995)

The RAF and Me: Wartime Memories of a Stirling Navigator 1941-1946 by Gordon Frost (pub. 2000)

Internet

Invasion of Java (1811) - wikipedia.org

Chief Maqoma: South African History Online - sahistory. org.za

Transkei: South African History Online - sahistory.org.za

Young Boy - A Country Childhood - pbs.org

History: University of Fort Hare - ufh.ac.za

General Information and History of Ciskei - ciskei.com

MOD St Athan - wikipedia.org

Early History of Aviation in the Eastern Province - ajol.info

List of British Commonwealth Air Training Plan Facilities in South Africa - wikipedia.org

Burma Star Association - burmastar.org.uk

Burma 1942 - history.army.mil

Rationing in the United Kingdom - wikipedia

Shy but Not Retiring: Memoirs Eric Kemp - books.google.
co.uk
Apartheid - wikipedia.org

National Archives
S.A.A.F Secret War Diary No. 44 Air School Grahamstown -
January-April 1943

Fort Beaufort Museum
History of the Museum
Alice
Hogsback
Fort Michel
Healdtown
Fort Fordyce
Balfour
Maqoma Heritage Route
General J.C. Smuts - Dingaans Day 1933

12896178R00102

Printed in Great Britain
by Amazon.co.uk, Ltd.,
Marston Gate.